Tai Chi Ch'uan

And the

I' Ching

Ben Noma, Sifu

Ben Noma, Sifu
Little Heaven Taiji Feng Shui
May 2018
Seattle, Washington

Tai Chi

and the

I' Ching

A guided imagery into the

Chi-energy

behind

Tai Chi Ch'uan

Taiji

The WAY you can go isn't the Real WAY
the NAME you can say isn't the Real NAME

Lao Tzu TAO TE CHING
-Ursula K. Le Guin *translation*

I Ching · 易經 · [yì jīng]

The Book of Changes · 64 Hexagrams

(The King Wen Sequence)

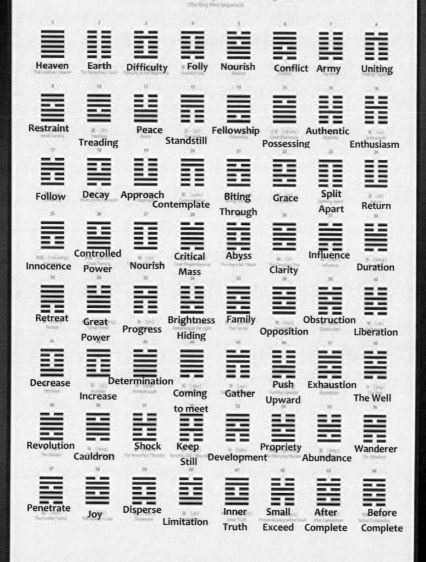

Heaven	Earth	Difficulty	Folly	Nourish	Conflict	Army	Uniting
Restraint	Treading	Peace	Standstill	Fellowship	Possessing	Authentic	Enthusiasm
Follow	Decay	Approach	Contemplate	Biting Through	Grace	Split Apart	Return
Innocence	Controlled Power	Nourish	Critical Mass	Abyss	Clarity	Influence	Duration
Retreat	Great Power	Progress	Brightness Hiding	Family	Opposition	Obstruction	Liberation
Decrease	Increase	Determination	Coming to meet	Gather	Push Upward	Exhaustion	The Well
Revolution	Cauldron	Shock	Keep Still	Development	Propriety	Abundance	Wanderer
Penetrate	Joy	Disperse	Limitation	Inner Truth	Small Exceed	After Complete	Before Complete

INTRODUCTION

Tai Chi Ch'uan is a practical Taoist art for longevity, self-defense and self-discipline. Tai chi ch'uan is moving meditation.

With this book, I am not explaining tai chi ch'uan. I am merely recognizing a chi-energy manifesting in all things and the information it carries, producing in our instance tai chi postures. I will attempt to write about the inspiration of that chi-energy. I am not a scholar, what I present is experience distilled into thoughts.

It is true that with regular practice, Tai Chi Ch'uan promotes deep abdominal breathing, tones the heart, improves digestion and makes strong kidneys. It gives oneself good balance and strong legs for excellent support. Tai chi ch'uan postures, shapes, sequence and choreography has trained mind and body. Now you have mastered the thirteen kinetic postures and coordinated the five steps with eight directions. Plus you have balance and learned to relax. But what compels nei gong practice long into old age? And you may ask, "what has the I' Ching to do with tai chi ch'uan? And why should I care? "

We have all observed women and men without particularly great strength or of small stature effortlessly perform super-normal deeds under great duress. The extraordinary example of a young mother saving her baby lifts a car. Fitness guru Jack Lalanne, over seventy years old, could swim while towing 70 boats across Lake Washington and 1033 push-ups in 23 minutes.

We have all observed women and men without particularly great strength or of small stature effortlessly perform super-normal deeds under great duress. The extraordinary example of a young mother saving her baby lifts a car. Fitness guru Jack Lalanne, over seventy years old, could swim while towing 70 boats across Lake Washington and perform 1033 push-ups in 23 minutes.

You may have experienced that while pushing hands, large, heavy stronger players seem to easily use their weight and mass to shove and knock you off balance. What is missing? So, how do the great Masters of Tai Chi Ch'uan perform such wonderful martial feats against strong opponents with so little effort as my teachers Dr. Tao Ping-Siang or Grandmaster William C.C. Chen demonstrated?

Power has the ability to produce a result; powerful has the ability to produce a result with little effort. Power carries information and behind information is chi-energy. Power can be achieved I believe by cultivating Sprit, Heart and Mind. Trusting you have the support of HEAVEN and EARTH, one can WARD-OFF on coming force.

'You can only win if you attack!' Say the pugilist.

You will find a central principal in Tai Chi Ch'uan practice: you cannot offend another. One can ONLY DEFEND ONESELF. A third alternative to fight or flight is to take a position of neutrality.

For tai chi players it is considered rude, bad practice to purposely cause harm. Even that little extra push or pull you do to prove yourself, is prideful. Mutual peace is neutral. Dr. Tao would say; 'Yield first, don't push back, and don't pull away' and 'not by force'! And Prof. Cheng Man Ching would counsel for an 'investment in loss'. Grandmaster Wm. CC Chen tells me, 'soften'.

A word of caution: Tai Chi or Bagua as defensive practice may end with injury to your opponent depending on the incoming force, so have care issuing energy.

Tai Chi Ch'uan & the I' Ching explores benefits to practicing Tai Chi Ch'uan. I believe each tai chi posture is a full expression of YANG energy before transmuting to YIN, in its continuous flow to the next posture, pausing momentarily passing through the experience of central equilibrium. Combined ideas provided by I' Ching that each hexagram expression is concretized until the next transformation line.

Thumb through the lessons, experience being plumb. Each time you may discover something else in the tai chi structure, or I' Ching structure, I encourage reading and research that broadens our minds enriching your experience.

The stated goal of Tai Chi Ch'uan is immortality, and Taoist ideas promoting health and longevity seek to follow a natural ways.   The I' Ching can aid by informing our understanding, tempering or exciting our feelings. Combining tai chi and I' Ching, we have a formula or equation for composure; being centered, and balanced. Balance is harmony. Harmony is resonance. Resonance brings empowerment.

Internal schools of martial arts are called nei gong. Tai chi ch'uan, chi gong, wu xing, tsing I, Bagua and le Hu Ba Fa are sister arts emerging from Taoist philosophies.   These schools cultivate health with methods of breathing and meditation. Thus reducing stress, relaxing our nervous systems, stimulating endocrine system and fortify immune system.

茓　燮 (手上) 33

Nei Gong, the internal art or soft style, involve using your mind to lead your practice and creation of internal sensing, feelings, and situational awareness. I' Ching provides insight, intuition for your mind, a holistic perception of life.

Tai chi ch'uan has a natural fluid motion and should feel as if you had been dancing. When the body moves well it is eloquent and graceful.

In the defense of tai chi as an aid in our modern times, and since we do not have the luxury of six to ten hours practice. Tai chi can still relieve stress caused by jobs, occupations, family, friends or whatever creates demands on our attention and occupies our time. Self-neglect, most commonly lack of sleep, can put an immense toll on our psycho-physical systems.

Solving the demands of modern life we brave mega-malls and supermarkets to hunt and gather super foods and exercise equipment and props and supports. Anxiously you gather provisions for shelter, food clothing, transportation and communication. It really is the day-to-day stuff that wears on us. Your modern life, your health and emotional well-being are being sacrificed on alters of production and progress.

It is the day to day stuff of life that wears on us. But stress is merely life pinching and poking you letting you know you are alive. I find three types of stress: distress, performance stress and low stress.

Distress can lead to poor performance and an inability to confront uncomfortable situations well, i.e. paralysis. Your mind is distracted and blood pressure rises.

Performance stress is exhilarating. Consider an athlete before a meet, or musician before a recital; both trained and confident to tackle any competition or performance. There is improved alertness, accompanied by rise in heart rate, nervousness and anxiety.

Low stress meditation, chi gong, tai chi practice; where the mind is calm and heart rate is normal, and self is composed.

Patterned movements or forms can be described as cause and effect. *But I' Ching and Tai Chi seem synchronistic, not causal.* I' Ching and Tai Chi continually flow with an innate sense to change direction should you encounter resistance or obstruction. In other words, whoever invented the I' Ching prepared for chance. Tai chi had great wisdom adapting it to a combat art.

Every day processes are partially or totally interfered with by chance. So much so that under normal circumstances, a normal course of events that conform to specific laws are almost an exception.

Tai Chi Ch'uan is not a fighting art, per se. But I do believe tai chi ch'uan, pushing hands or tui shou and all empty hands fighting should be t using Tai Chi Ch'uan shadow boxing.

Pushing Hands teaches relationship, our sensitivity and empathy for severity and passions.

For a non-combative two-person practice, tui shou can keep people off you. Discover sensitivity knowing your opponent but more importantly know yourself. To further your martial skills, a fighting application of your choice should also be learned.

A hexagram belonging to I' Ching and a tai chi posture both have structure and shape, a form. Where there is form there is information and behind information is chi-energy.

To assemble or construct good form we require quality chi-energy. Our thoughts and feelings breathe, stand in your own two feet, balanced, in essence tai chi ch'uan composure.

The cultivation of health and well-being through mindful thoughts and actions are achieved I believe in the daily practice of tai chi ch'uan and reading I' Ching. I' Ching stimulates our intuition, strengthening character, judgement and offers good conduct. Tai chi won't surrender our health and safety.

Take 20 minutes a day practice tai chi ch'uan and breathe. You will be rewarded with a strong body and alert mind.

I hope you enjoy this energetic approach to the multi-faceted yet simple and wonderful art of Tai Chi Ch'uan.

As a side note, I' (yi) translates to meaning the mind, Ching (jing) as change. I' Ching or 'Yi Jing direct translation is mind change.

Ben Noma
Seattle, 2020

I' Ching

*Heaven and earth and the ten thousand
things are born of being.
Being is born of no-thing.*

-Tao Te Ching

Brief History of I' Ching

The Taoist I' CHING is one of the oldest books in the world. China has had a continuous culture dating back 4717 years. The I' Ching, also known as the Book of Oracles, the Book of Wisdom, and the Book of Changes, is associated with ineffable Tao.

The I' Ching has sixty four hexagrams; a hexagram is created by combining two of 8-trigrams surrounding a bagua. I' Ching displays its ideas through the hexagrams' changing lines, carrying with it manifold meanings.

Four men are credited with authoring the I' Ching. 5000 years ago when humanity still hunted and gathered, the legendary **Fu Hsi** (?) by studying heaven, nature, animal tracks and even his own body, devised the yes/no , broken/unbroken lines to describe fundamental actions of nature. **Fu Hsi** is also associated with inventing cooking and herbalism.

While imprisoned by Emperor Shing Chu, **King Wen** (?) composed his book during his fifteen years in captivity. King Wen wrote the current form of hexagrams and philosophical commentaries, judgements and decisions still applied today. His son, the **Chuang Chou** (350-320 A.D.) added text pertaining to the individual lines. This became known and **Chuang Tzu Tao Te Ching**. Another anonymous product known as **Lao-Tzu** (which means 'Old Master', 'Old Philosopher') come to be known as the Lao Tzu's **Tao Te Ching**.

Confucius (551-479 B.C.) who wrote a complete and detailed philosophy associated with judgements and commentaries which have had lasting influences on the Chinese culture for a thousand years.

The internet is replete with I' Ching information. I believe the I' Ching, Bagua and Tai Chi are in danger of being lost to superstition; increasingly removed from nature, not adhering to original precepts that do not follow natural law and not being grounded by personal experience.

TRIGRAMS

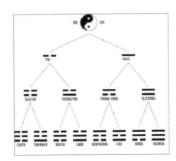

Trigrams are at the heart of I' Ching. Trigrams share three lines. The trigram represents an elemental force. On the bagua there are 8-trigrams. Because the 8-trigrams have differing structures and meanings associated; we can look at the chi-energy interpreted through their structures. Interpreted thus nature is at work and elements combine and withdraw, producing the myriad world around us.

The ancients began with a solid singular line for **Yes** —, a **YANG** line, and a broken line indicating **NO** — —, a **YIN** line…

…And in their wisdom added a third line, balancing the sacred geometry and three lines added to the bagua (eight trigrams).

Author Katya Walter in her wondrous book; the TAO of CHAOS, DNA AND THE I' CHING, says that "to learn the I' Ching expands the minds boundaries. How could one possibly code anything more universally, simply, and economically than with Yang and Ying?"

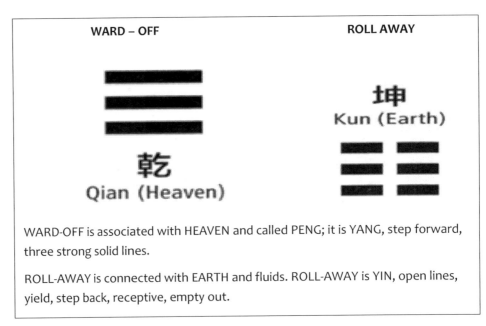

WARD-OFF is associated with HEAVEN and called PENG; it is YANG, step forward, three strong solid lines.

ROLL-AWAY is connected with EARTH and fluids. ROLL-AWAY is YIN, open lines, yield, step back, receptive, empty out.

Intrinsic energy pattern for trigram HEAVEN

乾
Qian (Heaven)

Name …… Trigram Ch'ien is **Heaven** or Celestial

Element ……….Metal

Taiji posture … Peng or Ward off

Shape ……….Round, sphere

Color ………..White, Dark red

Taste ………… Spicy, strong, pungent

Sensory Organ …… Nose

Characteristics …… Creative, great power, precision projection, elucidate, timed & order.

Place ………..the Sky, highlands, Stars

Astrology …….Boar & dog

Season ……… Autumn, early winter

Nature ……… Heaven is dynamic and strong, Father, King

HEAVEN possesses celestial nature with great stability. A cosmos trusting that all is unfolding as it should.   The mind is its own place, and in itself can make a Heaven of hell or Hell of heaven. *Milton (17c poet)*

    For Tai Chi players: head feels as though a golden thread from the sky lifts the crown of your skull, with tongue touching your upper palate with your chin tucked-in slightly. Chest and arms maintain circular, round, flexible shape.

Intrinsic energy pattern for EARTH trigram

Kun (Earth)

Name .... Trigram Kun is **Earth**, GAIA

Element .... Water

Taiji posture ...Lu, Roll away

Shape .... Square, rectangular

Color .... Black, dark red

Taste .... Sweet

Sensory Organ ... ... Ear, Dantien

Characteristic ...... Fecund, stable, nourishing, caring, supporting, grounding, entropy, decay, yielding, smooth.

Place .... Field, open space, rural

Astrology .... Sheep, ram

Season .... Late summer, early autumn

Nature .... Magnetic, devoted, Queen, Mother

EARTH is nurturing, an environment promoting fecundity. EARTH is receptive and mutable, yet supporting and firm.

For Tai Chi players: Mind, body spirit are grounded. Chest and arms maintain circular, round, flexible shape. Be aware of spine alignment to center (dantien), let SPIRIT rise from coccyx via spine to crown.

Intrinsic energy pattern for THUNDER

震
Zhen (Thunder)

Name ... ... Trigram Chen is **Thunder**

Element .....Wood

Taiji posture ...... Li, Split

Shape ....Square, void , roll, empty inside, uncovered

Color .... Green & yellow

Taste .... Salty

Sensory Organ.........Eye

Characteristic ... Arousing, active, excited, angry, nervous, shocking, threatening, quick, agile, sharp, alert

Place ....Hardwood, dense forests

Astrology ....Rabbit

Season ....Late Spring, early Summer

Nature ....Splitting, sudden awe, shock. oldest son or brother, warrior

THUNDER possesses an arousing nature, shock and awe. Rapid expansion, pressure compelling action.

For Tai Chi players: Heart is like an alert cat sensing a mouse; quick nimble, sharp, acute and sensitive.

Intrinsic energy pattern for WATER

坎
⼁ Kan (Water)

Name ………… Trigram Kan is **Water**

Element ……….Water

Taiji posture …Ji, Press

Shape …………….Wavy

Color …………..Black, dark red

Taste …….…...Salt, sour

Sensory Organ……….. Ears

Characteristic …………the Abyss, dangerous, ideas, expansion, privacy, mystery, cascade, fall, drip, flow

Place ………….Low, wet, swamp, pond, Sea

Organ ………...Ears, blood, kidney

Astrology …Rat

Season ……Winter

Nature, trouble, water is danger, clouds, rain, the middle son

WATER is nurturing and supportive. Mysterious and fathomless water is. Water carries information. WATER occupies low places on earth. I' Ching calls WATER the Abyss.

For Tai Chi players: Crown lifted by heaven, your arms should cascade from shoulders, carried by trunk of your body. No effort made to lift the limbs. There is a sense of spiraling, sinking but not weighted.

Intrinsic energy pattern of MOUNTAIN

Gen (Mountain)

Name ...... Trigram Ken is **Mountain**

Element .... Earth, stone, clay

Taiji posture .... Kao, Shoulder strike

Shape .... Round or Square

Color .... Dark yellow

Taste .... Sweet

Sensory Organ .... Mouth

Characteristic . .... Stand still, resist, withstand, stop, impede, slow, secretive, tough stubborn, empty inside but covered

Place .... Temples, churches, office buildings

Astrology .... Ox

Season .... Late Winter & early Spring

Nature .... stand still

MOUNTAIN refers to stillness and stopping, quiet and composed; arresting incorrect and inappropriate action. MOUNTAIN stillness is pervasive inside and outside. Composure and transformation through stillness.

For Tai Chi players: Head held at crown, tongue pushes upper palette, slightly lift coccyx. Chest and arms maintain circular, round, flexible shape. Hearts of your palms lift/push out gently.

Intrinsic energy patterns of WIND/WOOD

Xun (Wind)

Name ………...Trigram Sun is **Wind & Wood**

Element ……..Wood

Taiji Posture …...Tsai, Pull Down

Shape …….……..Vertical, straight up

Color ……....…... Blue, white

Taste …………...Salty

Sensory Organ....Eye

Characteristic ….Growth, penetrating, gentle

Place …….…….. Dense wood, forests

Astrology ……...Dragon, snake

Season ………....Spring

Nature ………... Wind is the gentle, penetrating,
wind belongs to wood, youngest daughter

WOOD and WIND are interchangeable, wood promote growth, wind is expansive, nurturing and versatile. WIND is fierce like cyclone or a gentle penetrating wind. WOOD and WIND are Yin forms, and soft and pliable, but sometimes Yang energy which is sturdy.

For Tai Chi players: Body and arms are flexible, curving like a crescent moon, relaxed kua (flexible waist), and strong but resilient legs. Internal energy circulates and flows without interruption.

Intrinsic energy pattern of FIRE

離
)   Li (Fire)

Name ...... Trigram Li is **Fire**

Element .... Fire

Taiji posture........ Li, Push

Shape .... Triangle

Color .... Red, bright red

Taste .... Bitter

Sensory Organ........ Tongue

Characteristic ...... Light giving, hot, enlightened, beautiful, embrace, hold, carry, control agitated, sticky, clinging, consuming, extrovert.

Place.....................Temples, churches, office buildings

Astrology ....Horse

Season .... Summer

Nature .... Fire is clinging, chaos, sun, the Middle-daughter,

FIRE comes from the south and brings heat. It is the forces of summer. FIRE is the pulse in the body.

For Tai Chi players: Compose your Heart, a tranquil Mind and lively Spirit are held or embraced in the dantien.

Intrinsic energy pattern of LAKE

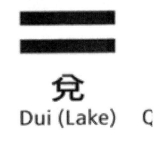

Dui (Lake)   ੮

Name ……..Trigram Tui is **Lake**

Element ……..Metal

Taiji posture …Zhou, Elbow stroke

Shape……….Oval

Color ………..White, purple

Taste ………..Hot, spicy

Sensory Organ…….Nose

Characteristic ……Joy, pleasure, happy, laughing, lock-up control, restrain, water surrounded by land

Place ……….Marsh, pond, river bank, pool, basin

Astrology …..Rooster

Season ……...Autumn

Nature …….. Lake is joyous, pooling, gathering

LAKE represents autumn and maturity. LAKE is gathering and containment. The element metal is associated with LAKE, dogmatic and resolute. Positive side is strong and intuitive, negative side is inflexible and melancholic.

For Tai Chi players: Mouth is closed, teeth do not touch. Tip of tongue push against palate. Breathe from nostrils into your dantien. Your mouth will produce thin sweet saliva.

Bagua

Heaven and earth act as bellows: Empty yet structured it moves,
inexhaustibly giving.
                                              -Tao te Ching

Bagua, Tai Chi and I' Ching correlations

良
Gen (Mountain)

CENTRAL EQUILIBRIUM: Imagine **HEAVEN** (bai hui) as your **upward force**, propelled by focusing your mind on the crown of your head.   Simultaneously your feet are firm, weight centered. Head, neck and spine are aligned. Still and composed.

坎
Kan (Water)

PRESS: Focus your minds attention on a **downward spiral**; sink like **WATER** into your belly (dantien).

離
Li (Fire)

PUSH: With a firm root, energize palms (lao gong) three fingers push out issuing an **entering force** expanding, clinging like **FIRE**.

坤
Kun (Earth)

ROLL AWAY: Coiling into your center gives a **yielding backward force** toward **EARTH** (meng men).

震
Zhen (Thunder)

SHOULDER/ELBOW STROKE: Sitting in your (sung kwa) legs issues **right and left force**.

Center, right, left, forward and back are illustrated on the bagua when read with mindfulness and is heartfelt. Building Hexagrams further reveals the correlation between Tai Chi Ch'uan and the I' Ching.

Trigrams to Hexagrams

Hexagrams have SIX lines; one trigram on top and another trigram below. Our example below, Hexagram 63 is what the I' Ching calls AFTER COMPLETION can mean finished business.

The top trigram is **WATER**, lines 4,5,6.

And the bottom trigram is **FIRE**, lines 1,2,3.

Combining trigrams **WATER** over **FIRE** produces Hexagram 63 which the I' Ching calls **'AFTER COMPLETION'**. Notice the solid foundation followed by alternating lines of compression and flex.

Hexagram 63 called 'AFTER **COMPLETION'**

Water (lines 4,5,6) on top

FIRE (lines 1,2,3) at bottom

WATER over **FIRE** produces an image of a boiling a pot or cauldron over fire and may be interpreted as very energetic or spirited activity. Something done with exuberance.

Hexagram 63 means completed, already past, state of perfection, equilibrium and harmony.

It is either highly coincidental or very synchronistic that hidden within Hexagram 64 is another hexagram relaying information associated with the hexagram we a working with!

The nuclear hexagram produces 'BEFORE COMPLETION' meaning unfinished business. The top trigram is now FIRE, lines 3, 4, & 5. And below is the trigram WATER, lines 2, 3, & 4 combined the two trigrams produce Hexagram 64 and FIRE over WATER the I' Ching calls 'BEFORE COMPLETION'.

FIRE over WATER is not a stable condition, energy is extinguished. It is opposite of hexagram 63 we started with. Notice its weak foundation line and unsupported heavy lines. Hexagram 64 feels less stable.

Our new Hexagram 64 the I' Ching calls 'BEFORE COMPLETION'

FIRE (lines 4, 5, 6) top

WATER (lines 1, 2, 3) below

FIRE over WATER produces image of extinguishing. Ironically, Hexagram 64 BEFORE COMPLETION is translated to mean unfinished business, indicating work to be done, perfection is temporary. A sort of reverse structure of our former Hexagram 63 'AFTER COMPLETION'.

Tai Chi Ch'uan also called shadow boxing, through its sequential choreography emulates the I' Ching eight trigram; the stillness that is a mountain, energetic as fire, flow like a river, shock & awe of thunder, calm (or tempestuous) as a lake.

Tai Chi postures enjoy firm foundations, central equilibrium, the support that is the strength of heaven and earth; but fluid and soft as water, and gentle as the wind.

As we move into, out of and between our Tai Chi shapes & postures, we carry intent through the posture. Why not carry the chi-energy of the I' Ching Hexagram 63 called AFTER COMPLETION, an image of boiling energy of water fueled by engine of fire.

Taoist Five-element theories provide the agents and mechanisms for much change in our world.

YIN/YANG theory provide constant assessment of the harmony and dissonance of our world.

I' Ching hexagrams carry information, contemplations for good behavior, and proper conduct.

Tai chi ch'uan practice and I' Ching energy resonate with the heart and mind and is expressed by throughout our body as health and vitality
.

I believe that the structure of a hexagram carries sufficient information e.g. THUNDER over MOUNTAIN; that the Tai Chi player may intuit its message and chi-energy from its changing lines and produce a tai chi shape. The hexagram itself reveals its strength and weaknesses, while revealing its unique character and resonance. This requires we employ a wholistic mind not sequential or linear.

The most obvious characteristic possessing Hexagram 1 called HEAVEN is its strength, its' solid lines. Trigram for HEAVEN is above and HEAVEN is also below, it appears very strong, exhibiting truly YANG qualities. Firm structure illustrated by solid unbroken lines.

WARD OFF is the tai chi posture for HEAVEN over HEAVEN and called peng (pronounced 'pung'). Peng exhibits cosmic strength, celestial movement, it is very strong, but its weakness is not yielding.

Exploring I' Ching this way, I think avoids intellectual pursuits of tai chi. Too much understanding, many thoughts lead to over producing tai chi shapes, forming habits resulting in struggle and effort, possible pain. Relax and breathe. Center yourself. Tai chi is felt; WARD OFF is supported by the strength of HEAVEN. Central Equilibrium is at work here: golden thread from heaven to crown, tip of tongue at upper palette, rooted on three nails.

Applying the I' Ching to tai chi ch'uan leaves your heart and mind free to play with the chi-energy behind the information producing your Tai Chi Ch'uan form.

尾雀撮右步上（手上）63

WARD-OFF

Apply I' Ching to Tai Chi

Take a look at Tai Chi Ch'uan **OPENING** or **BEGINNING** movement initiating the form , it is Hexagram 35, the trigram **FIRE** is on top of the trigram for **EARTH** which give us Hexagram 35 the I' Ching calls **PROGRESS**.

Hexagram 35
PROGRESS

FIRE over **EARTH** evokes an image of sunrise, of giving light or warmth, or a campfire, feeling safe.

The **OPENING** movement **FIRE** over **EARTH** (sunrise) the I' Ching calls **PROGRESS**.

In the OPENING movement our attention begins at the crown of head suspended by a golden thread from heaven, hollow the chest, dantien relaxed, fingers expanding/contracting to rhythm of breath while connected to three-nail root, and arms carried by trunk of body, a tranquil mind, peaceful heart and lively sprit.

THE SECOND POSTURE: BEGINNING FORM

1   2

Now let us take a close look at **SINGLE-WHIP.** This tai chi posture is Hexagram 49, **LAKE** (4 ,5 ,6) over **FIRE** (1, 2, 3). The I' Ching calls the energy of **SINGLE WHIP,** REVOLUTION**.**

Combining **LAKE** over **FIRE** provokes an image of a lake of lava, which is extremely awesome energy; a dynamo; an image of unbridled energy, attractive magnetic & sticky. LAKE over FIRE is a cauldron of liquid, living earth.

SINGLE WHIP is **REVOLUTION** and does not matter if the spin energy is centripetal or centrifugal; it is an instance of spinning, an orbit; change is in the air; also called metamorphosis, transformation and sometimes called the love hexagram for radical change.

SINGLE WHIP is **REVOLVING**, a Coriolis effect, a cyclone; the calm is at the center vortex while centrifugal forces create shear power.

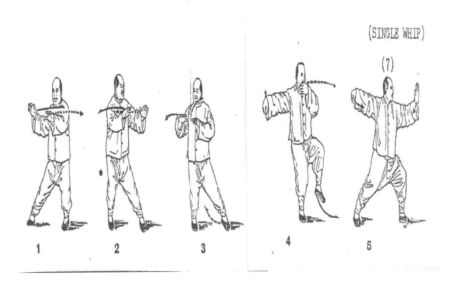

(SINGLE WHIP)

(7)

1   2   3   4   5

Hexagrams have embedded them another hexagram. An interesting phenomenon occurs during the bagua transformations, the I' Ching recognizes that imbedded within hexagrams are nuclear hexagrams.

We have learned that hexagrams are embedded within a hexagram. An interesting phenomenon during the transformations of the bagua and the I' Ching recognizes that phenomena.

Let's use our example, Tai chi posture SINGLE WHIP,   Hexagram 49 possessing two trigrams **LAKE** over **FIRE**.

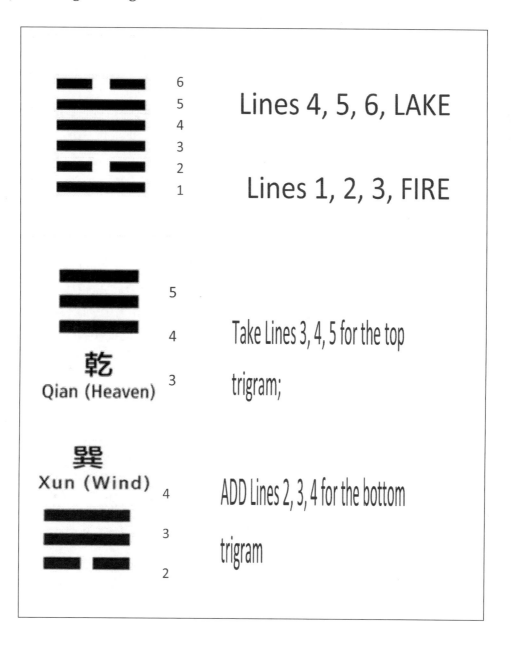

Nested within is **TEMPTATION,** Hexagram 44 embedded within our SINGLE **WHIP,** Chi-energy residing in this tai chi posture is illustrated by two trigrams **HEAVEN** over **WIND**. The I' Ching calls this **TEMPTATION.**

Hexagram 44
Temptation

The hexagrams structure appears solid but it is built on an untenable broken linea change line. The firm yang lines may entice one to think it indestructible; but based on the singular broken line at its foundation, the energy alludes to desire, enticement or seduction, and it gives another layer of mystery regarding the chi-energy of its host Hexagram 49, SINGLE WHIP.

TEMPTATION is an encounter with primal forces, can be interpreted as not controlling unruly passions or give into folly. It may be very tempting to use force here, to push and pull when executing SINGLE WHIP, but think it through.

Author D. F Hook comments on the I' Ching Hexagram 44, and says this hexagram contains '*a definite warning about a person or situation which may appear harmless but will prove dangerous*'

My point is that behind the posture **SINGLE WHIP** is information about **HEAVEN, WIND,** something **REVOLVING** and **TEMPTATION,** information carried by its two hexagrams, which seems to warn that correct posture and attitude are required to produce and execute Tai Chi posture **SINGLE WHIP.**

尾打左步撇(手上)11

Bagua

Mysterious power goes deep. It reaches far. It follows things back, clear back to the great oneness.

-Tao te Ching

Moving in Space

Form School feng shui approaches the bagua from an energetic point of view, ignoring the myriad superstitions associated today with feng shui and bagua. But you can read the energy reflected in bagua. Trigrams structures carry its unique information, similar to no two snowflakes or fingerprints or crystals or sunrises are the same. Moving in space is in real time, as you read this, time and space has just moves on, I Ching.

Bagua translated means eight trigrams; literally (ba) means eight and (gua) is word for trigram. Each of eight trigrams revolve through 360 degrees in any and all directions within a sphere.

In 1990, Tai Chi Master Paul Crompton wrote; *"If we take the I' Ching's description of the eight trigrams, we have the attributes of Strong, Yielding, Inciting-movement, Dangerous, Resting, Penetrating, Light-giving, Joyful;* ideas corresponding to bagua images of Heaven, Earth, Thunder, Water, Mountain, Wind, Fire and Lake.

1. Ch'ien	HEAVEN	Ward-off
2. Sun	WIND	Pull –down
3. Kan	WATER	Press
4. Ken	MOUNTAIN	Shoulder-stroke
5. Kun	EARTH	Roll away
6. Chen	THUNDER	Split
7. Li	FIRE	Push
8. Tui	LAKE	Elbow-stroke

Tai Chi Ch'uan and the Thirteen Kinetic Postures

There is one trigram for each of **eight compass headings'** on earth or directions. The **five steps** are your positions. Let's explore the five-steps in detail.

Together they characterize the bagua and are the thirteen kinetic postures of Tai chi Ch'uan.

The **8 Directions or gates** correlate to eight tai chi postures.

4 cardinal gates (directions)

1. **North**.....Peng ....Ward-off ....Ch'ien.......Heaven
2. **South**..... Lu .... .Roll-away......... Kun........ ....Earth
3. **East**...... Ji ....Press .... Kan ....Water
4. **West** ....An .... Push ....Li ....Fire

4 diagonal gates (directions)

5. **Northeast** ... Tsai. ... Pull-down ... ...Sun .... Wind
6. **Southeast** ....Kao ....Shoulder .... Ken ....Mountain
7. **Northwest**.....Zhou...Elbowstrike ...Tui .... Lake
8. **Southwest**..... Li..... .Split ....Chen ....Thunder

The sequence for **Five Steps** is called 'grasps the sparrows tail' and correlate to the core movement of tai chi shapes.

1. Central Equilibrium	Center
2. Step Forward	Ward Off
3. Step Back	Roll Back
4. Step Right	Press
5. Step Left	Push

Operating within a sphere, the **eight directions** plus the **five steps** are called the **Thirteen Kinetic Postures of Tai Chi Ch'uan.**

Coordination, Balance & Proportion

In this bagua, the eight trigrams are well balanced surrounding the eight directions as they spin through the directions. Each trigram is in proportion to its opposite; where Heaven (North) is over Earth (South). Fire in the West is balanced by Water in the East.

Coordination, balance and proportion are the result of the five steps. Master Henry Huang of Comox, Vancouver Island B.C has seven principles for tai chi. All of which should be attended to, particularly coordination, balance and proportion. Be mindful of proportion. Proportion is crucial to Tai Chi players. Proportion gives balance to the center. Shoulders coordinated to hips, wrist to ankles, knees to elbows, and head to spine. Example would be Tai Chi posture Brush Knee; the heart of your right palm (laogong) is coordinated to the bubbling well of your left foot (yong quon).

Tai Chi Ch'uan movements are coordinated to the eight directions. Multiply the eight directions by eight trigrams 8X8 produces 64 Hexagrams contained within the I' Ching.

Tai Chi posture **'PICK UP NEEDLE AT SEA BOTTOM'** is **THUNDER** over **MOUNTAIN**, producing Hexagram 62 which means **PREPONDERENC OF THE SMALL**. Its structure looks untenable.

Tai Chi posture **'PICK UP NEEDLE AT SEA BOTTOM'** is **Thunder** over **Mountain,** producing **Hexagram 62** which means PREPONDERENC OF THE SMALL. Its structure looks untenable.

PICK UP NEEDLE AT SEA BOTTOM displays the chi-energy for Hexagram 62. This posture follows the yielding compression below and splitting energy above, exhibiting core strength.

Thunder over Mountain, Hexagram 62 signals a transition, the I' Ching calls it the **PREPONDERANCE of the SMALL,** information regarding success through small beginnings.

Let's explore the five steps as it is applied to tai chi ch'uan.

'Grasp sparrow's tail: the FIVE STEPS

step (1)

Center

*Song of Central Equilibrium

脚分方（步换）身轉（手上）55

We are centered, stable and still as a mountain.

Our *ch'I* sinks to the tan-tien

we are as if suspended from above.

Our spirit is concentrated within and

our outward manner perfectly composed.

Receiving and issuing energy are both the work of an instant.

*text ref: Douglas Wile, Yang Family Secret Transmissions

'Grasp sparrow's tail: the FIVE STEPS

Step (2)

North

乾

Qian (Heaven)

Step FORWARD

PENG

Ward Off

*Song of WARD-OFF

尾雀揽右步上（手上）63

How do we explain the energy of ward-off?
It is like water which supports a moving boat.
First make the *ch'I* in the *tan-tien* substantial,
Then hold the head as if suspended from heaven.
The whole body has the power of a spring.
Opening and closing should be clearly defined.
Even if the opponent uses a thousand pounds of force.
We will float lightly and without difficulty.

*text ref: Douglas Wile, <u>Yang Family Secret Transmissions</u>

'Grasp sparrow's tail: the FIVE STEPS

坤
Kun (Earth)

Step (3)

South

Step BACK

LU

ROLL AWAY

*Song of ROLL-AWAY

揑步撒身轉（手下）20

How can we explain the energy of roll-back?
We draw the opponent towards us by allowing him to advance,
While we follow his incoming force.
Continuing to draw him in until he overextends,
We remain light and comfortable, no loss of vertical posture.
When his force is spent he will naturally be empty,
While we maintain our center of gravity, And never be bested by the opponent.

*text ref: Douglas Wile, Yang Family Secret Transmissions

'Grasp sparrow's tail: the FIVE STEPS

坎
Kan (Water)

Step (4)
EAST

Step RIGHT
JI
Press

*Song of PRESS

言左步上（手上）21

How can we explain the energy of press?
Sometimes we use two sides
To directly receive a single intention.
Meeting and combing in one movement.
We indirectly receive a ball bouncing off a wall,
Or a coin dropped on a drum,
Which bounces up with metallic sound.

*test ref: Douglas Wile, <u>Yang Family Secret Transmissions</u>

'Grasp sparrow's tail: the FIVE STEPS

Step (5)
WEST

Step LEFT
AN
Push

離
) Li (Fire)

*Song of PUSH

按 身 轉 （手下）14

How can we explain the energy of push?
When applied, it's like water in motion
But within its softness there is great strength.
When the flow is swift, the force cannot be withstood.
Meeting high places the waves break over them,
And encountering low places they dive deep.
The waves rise and fall,
And finding a hole they surely surge in.

*test ref: Douglas Wile, Yang Family Secret Transmissions

'What fear have we of an opponent's excellent technique?', asks tai chi classic 'Secret Applications of the Thirteen Postures'. And answers: "When an opponent closes in on us forcefully and strikes, we must evade by withdrawing our center and step aside."

Tai Chi Ch'uan

For a house, a good thing is level ground.

-Tao Te Ching

Brief History of Tai Chi Ch'uan and the I' Ching

Tai Chi's long and shadowy history defies accuracy; but it should be noted that Taoist meditations, Book I' Ching, YIN / YANG theory and Wu-Xing preceded Tai Chi Ch'uan by centuries if not millennia. The words "Tai Chi' can be translated to mean Grand Ultimate.

Sixth century India monk Sakyamuni, Gautama Buddha, and known to Chinese as Da Mo came to China to meditate. He initiated the Wu Tang and Shaolin schools, and exercises contributing to Tai Chi Ch'uan.

Followers of Da Mo, particularly the legendary fourteenth century Taoist alchemist monk Chang San-feng, a contemporary of Confucius, and both having strong interest in the Book I' Ching, is associated with making the greatest contributions to Tai Chi Ch'uan.

*According to legend, while meditating Chang Seng-Feng saw a snake and crane locked in mortal combat. The crane would attack the snake's head with its sword like beak, but the snake would turn its head aside and attacked the crane's neck, the crane would use its wing to protect its neck, the snake darts for the crane's leg and it's left wing wards off the attack. Stabbing again and again, the crane was not able to make a solid strike. After tiring of the fight, the Crane flew away and the Snake slithered off resting in preparation for their next encounter.

Chang San-feng realized from their performance the living principal of the I' Ching; the strong changing to the soft and the becoming strong. Soft overcomes hard. Coursing water wears away stone, yet always yielding.

From watching animals, clouds, trees, and even his own body, Master Chang San-feng codified these actions into White Crane Spread its Wings, Snake Creeps Down, Brush Knee & Push, Roll-away & ward off. His desire was that the whole world attains longevity, not merely martial skills.

Finally the recluse Chang San-feng found solitude on Wu-tang Mountain and started the Wu-tang School.

The Song Dynasty (1150AD) added the Eight Brocades to the already archaic mediation movements to the creation of a martial application as described in the *Illustrated Exposition of Internal Techniques* (1882).

The nineteenth century found China pugilistic and fractured. It's Governance weakened by invading trade nations, Triad criminal organizations, over-population dominated by males, high unemployment and the opium wars.

During this time, many internal arts, Tai Chi Ch'uan, Bagua ch'uan, Xing I', Le Hu Ba Fa were taught, but only secretly, from Father to Son and to no one outside family, for fear it may fall into irresponsible hands. Family lessons were seldom written down, but once written they were treasured as family secrets. And 12th century Marshall Yue Fei added the Eight Brocade tai chi qigong to improve the 'vitality of his soldiers',

It was in this social climate that young Yang Lu-Chan (1799-1872) appropriated the much revered and secretly guarded Tai Chi Ch'uan from Ch'en Chan Hsing, Chen family village.

Yang Lu Chan went on to create a tai chi legacy for the Yang Family, and his grandson Yang Cheng Fu would later teach a most famous tai chi master Professor Cheng Man-Cheng, whose teachings reached millions of people around the world.

Wu Wei & Tai Chi & YING/YANG

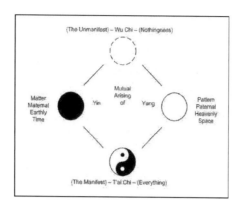

"The Tao does nothing, yet nothing is left undone."

Here is my clumsy attempt to describe this mystery. In the same manner that light is related to dark, Tai Chi and Wu Chi are related. Movement comes from stillness and returns. Wu chi is characterized as action through inaction. Wu chi has the quality of not-doing, yet things are accomplished. Wu chi is effortlessness, requiring that you do nothing in order for something to be accomplished. Wu chi lacks information, yet all the chi-energy is there for construction.

Before **Tai Chi** there is **Wu Chi.** Wu Chi refers to a state where there are no forms, where nothing-ness and everything-ness co-exist; movement/no movement, up/down, on/off etc. Where empty and full is one. Behind this dual one-ness lies chi-energy regardless if in movement or stillness: before yin and yang and before time and space; un-manifest. Before existence, all is connected and there "it" is indistinct, full of potential, raw chi-energy. Our familiar tai chi ball represents perfect balance.

 Tai Chi balance is illustrated with a black fish chasing a white fish. The idea represents our dual reality and a balance between them, such as, day and night, up and down, right or left. Within the white fish there is a black dot and white dot in the black fish; an idea that there is a bit of YANG in YING and vice versa. These are complimentary but opposing forces, juxtaposing tensions. YING and YANG can be viewed as balance between quality and quantity. An example may be a mountain that is lush with vegetation compared to a mountain that is barren.

Wu chi appears to be a collective consciousness, a sort of glue or plasma holding the universe together. Tai chi is the projections. Wu chi can be characterized by Center and Stillness. Tai Chi is movement and communication.

Imagine a single soccer ball in the immense infinity of all consuming space; 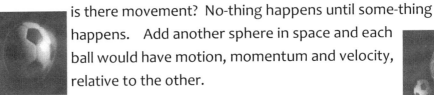 is there movement? No-thing happens until some-thing happens. Add another sphere in space and each ball would have motion, momentum and velocity, relative to the other.

Communication with one another is dependent on the ability to send and receive vibrations. We are connected by good vibration & bad vibration, as electromagnetic radiation. The chi-energy carried by our thoughts becomes actions, gestures and body language; whether overt or covert. Our perceptions and thoughts influence our behavior. Our bio-plasma informs us via chi-energy and we react for better or worse. Think good thoughts.

Tai chi movements are directed by the mind (chi-energy) and expressed through our body. Tai Chi pursued intellectually can take a long time, but energetically we quickly ascertain any intent behind fierce and rapid moves, and is felt first by your Heart/Mind; I believe the I' Ching names and meanings offers a glimpse on how to temper these feelings aiding Tai Chi Ch'uan solo and push hands practice.

Tai Chi Ch'uan
the Art of Practice

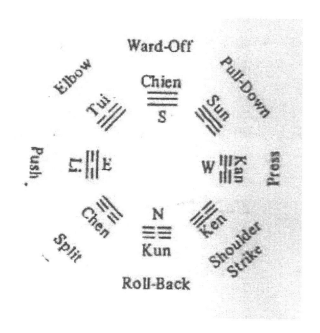

What's not the Way soon ends.

-Tao te Ching

Breathe

*

center yourself

*

Golden thread from heaven suspends crown of head

*

tuck chin in, tongue touches upper palette

*

bones plumb and stacked on ground
head square on shoulders

*

arms loose and cascade from shoulders

*

eyes half closed with diffused awareness

*

your mind to a tranquil place

*

peace in your heart

*

playful spirit

Preparation
Wu Chi

THE FIRST POSTURE: PREPARTORY POSTURE

Breathe

Opening move

Tai Chi Ch'uan's OPENING move has (trigram) FIRE over (trigram) EARTH resulting in Hexagram 35 I' Ching says is PROGRESS. Fire is enlightening and Earth receptive, an image of giving light. Sun rising over the planet is progress. Imagine a campfire, and warm comfort with a bit of excitement. Hexagram 39 displays compressed earth connecting consuming energy above. Hexagram 35 BEGINNING is compact and yielding has hidden sticky rising strength.

The inside nuclear Hexagram 39 is WATER over MOUNTAIN, and means OBSTRUCTION, the I' Ching describes it to mean inaccessible.

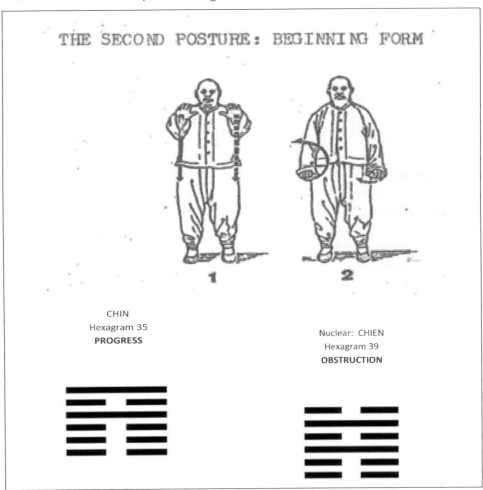

THE SECOND POSTURE: BEGINNING FORM

1   2

CHIN
Hexagram 35
PROGRESS

Nuclear: CHIEN
Hexagram 39
OBSTRUCTION

Fire over Earth is Progress

Ward Off –PENG Grasp sparrow's tail

Tai chi posture WARD-OFF or PENG (pronounced 'pung') is Hexagram 1 combining HEAVEN over HEAVEN, the Celestial. The everlasting SKY is uncompromising, immovable, unwavering. Movement of HEAVEN is powerful, strong and dynamic. "True nature and destiny comes to permanence through perseverance and Great Harmony". Hexagram 1 HEAVEN/WARD-OFF is the steadfast strength of Heaven.

Hidden inside the nuclear Hexagram 1 is also Heaven. Allow your mind lead.

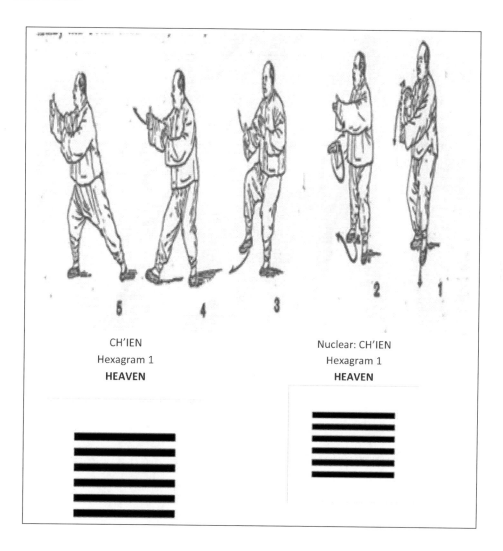

CH'IEN
Hexagram 1
HEAVEN

Nuclear: CH'IEN
Hexagram 1
HEAVEN

Heaven is called the Creative

Roll Away – LU Grasp the sparrow's tail

ROLL-AWAY also called LU is Hexagram 2 EARTH. Earth is a water planet. Roll-away is the watercourse way; liquid expansion. Prefers to follow, occupies lowest spots, cautious, magnetic and penetrating. The condition is unforgiving and devoted to the receptive, allowing, and letting, flowing. If you lead you'll go astray. Hexagram 2 ROLL-AWAY is step back uses attractive magnetic hidden energy. What is meld?

Nuclear Hexagram 2 is also the Receptive. Yield first, don't pull away, and don't push back, never by force.

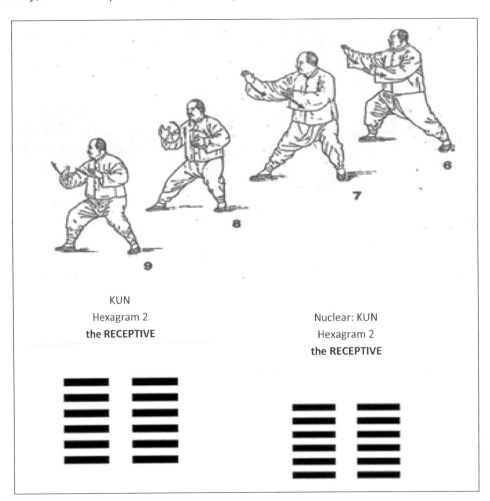

KUN
Hexagram 2
the RECEPTIVE

Nuclear: KUN
Hexagram 2
the RECEPTIVE

Earth is called the Receptive

Press – JI Grasp the sparrow's tail

Tai Chi posture Ji is PRESS is Hexagram 29 called the ABYSS characterized by WATER above and WATER below. The abyss is danger! An image of Water falling...abyss is downward, deep, ravine, pit, gulf, cavity, a crevasse. Water is content, to occupy the lowest places on earth. Hexagram 29, PRESS issues the ever increasing sinking pressure and weight of the abyss.

The nuclear Hexagram 27 is MOUNTAIN over THUNDER and looks like open jaws and is called CORNERS of the MOUTH, meaning

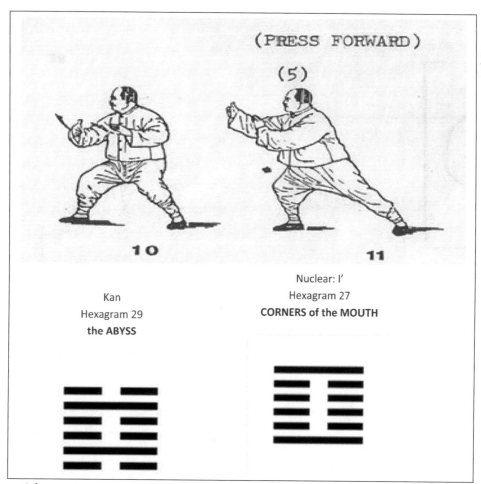

(PRESS FORWARD)

(5)

10

11

Kan
Hexagram 29
the ABYSS

Nuclear: I'
Hexagram 27
CORNERS of the MOUTH

nourishment.

Water is called the Abyss

Push – AN Grasp the sparrow's tail

Taiji posture PUSH, called AN, is Hexagram 30 FIRE over FIRE. Hexagram 28 the I' Ching calls the CLINGING. The Clinging is radiating and sticky. To-catch-on-fire, conflagrate, it is consuming, bold & fearless. PUSH contains Tai Chi sticky energy and dynamic perseverance. Success of clarity comes from correct attitude of body and mind. What is lift?

Nuclear Hexagram 28 is called PREPONDERANCE OF THE GREAT and carries a warning that things turn in on themselves. There is a tipping point once excess is reached.

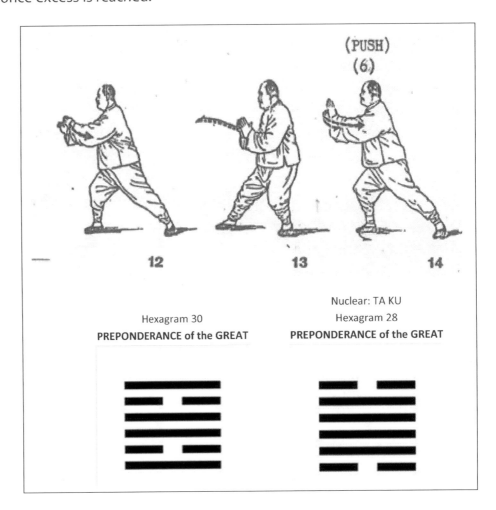

(PUSH)
(6.)

12   13   14

Hexagram 30
PREPONDERANCE of the GREAT

Nuclear: TA KU
Hexagram 28
PREPONDERANCE of the GREAT

Fire is called the Clinging

Single Whip

SINGLE WHIP is Hexagram 49. Lake over Fire the I' Ching calls revolution, and it invokes an image of a lava lake. Lake is called joyous and enjoys gathering, but fire brings tension. Fire is sticky energy, clinging, churning, agitating, and whipping. SINGLE Whips' dynamic coiling can be centrifugal or centripetal energy revolving around dantien.

The nuclear Hexagram 44 is ENCOUNTER, love, liaison or seduction. Trigrams HEAVEN over WIND bring caution of hidden influences from an alluring and furtive unseen danger, no ground to stand on. It is tempting to use force, to push and pull your opponent but proper central equilibrium and execution is required.

SINGLE WHIP is called **REVOLUTION**, the weight shifts are many, spinning 180 degrees; your center is the spindle, your arms give proportion

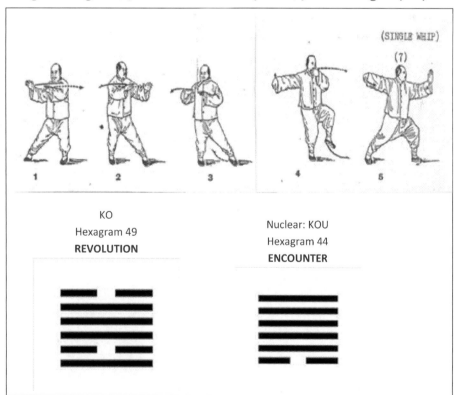

revolving under your head lifted at the crown.   How does Coriolis work?

Lake over Fire is called Revolution
Raise Hands

Tai chi posture RAISING HANDS like PLAY GUITAR has Hexagram 17 meaning FOLLOW. Hexagram 17 has THUNDER over LAKE. Thunder is movement and together with the metal and gathering of Lake, gives the images FOLLOW, adapting, conforming. Movement and joy like dancing are stimulating, exciting, enthusiastic, rousing, sensitive and loving. Hex 17 FOLLOW illustrates the splitting action. What is sticking?

The nuclear Hexagram 53 is DEVELOPMENT meaning gradual progress. Give special attention to central equilibrium.

(RAISE HANDS AND STEP UP)

(8)

1   2

SUI   Nuclear: CHIEN
Hexagram 17   Hexagram 53
FOLLOW   **DEVELOPMENT**

Lake over Thunder called Follow

Shoulder Stroke

SHOULDER STRIKE is Hexagram 34 called the Power of the Great! Thunder over Heaven.   Pressure is building up in heaven. Once aroused an image of gathering a storms...things do not retreat for ever. Hexagram 34 SHOULDER STROKE displays strength of heaven with shock and awe.

The nuclear Hexagram 43 is called BREAKTHROUGH meaning

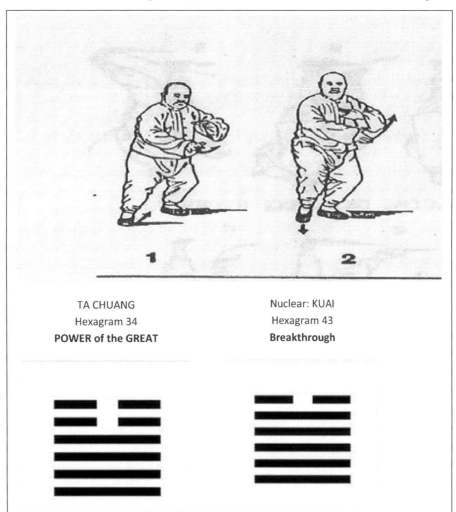

TA CHUANG
Hexagram 34
POWER of the GREAT

Nuclear: KUAI
Hexagram 43
Breakthrough

resoluteness. Let love happen, get out of your way.

Thunder over Heaven is Power of the Great

White Crane Spreads its Wings

WHITE CRANE SPREADS WINGS is Hexagram 22 MOUNTAIN over FIRE and called GRACE. An image of campfires at the foot of a mountain, visions of comfort, grace, poise, elegant, finesse, polite, decency, courtesy come to heart. Hex 22 STORK COOLS WINGS has stone exterior with uncompromising compressed resting strength.

The nuclear Hexagram 40 THUNDER over WATER means DELIVERANCE, difficulties resolved.

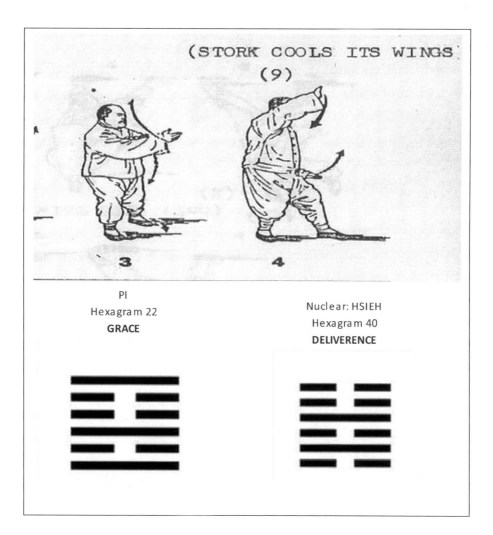

Mountain over Fire meaning Grace

Brush Knee & Push

Tai chi shape BRUSH THE KNEE AND PUSH is Hexagram 18 MOUNTAIN over WIND and means undertakings bring misfortune. Work on that which has been spoiled, stagnation, fixing and rectify misdeeds. Hexagram 18, TWIST STEP and BRUSH KNEE has the penetrating WIND delivering compressed, stillness, un-moving MOUNTAIN energy.

Inside, the nuclear Hexagram 54 arousing thunder over joyous lake carry a warning, the MARRYING MAIDEN means affection with caution.

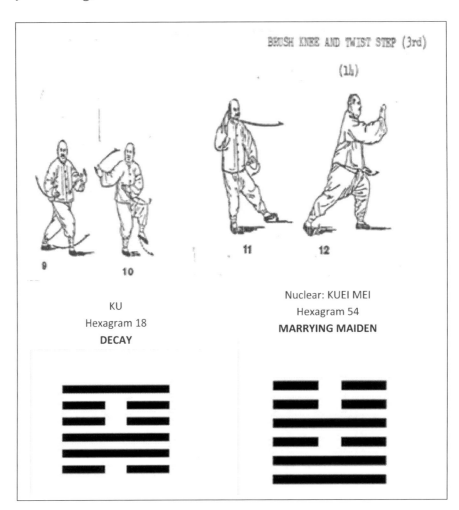

BRUSH KNEE AND TWIST STEP (3rd)

(14)

9
10

11
12

KU
Hexagram 18
DECAY

Nuclear: KUEI MEI
Hexagram 54
MARRYING MAIDEN

Mountain over Wind means Decay

Play Guitar

PLAY GUITAR, as with RAISE HANDS, we find Hexagram 17 LAKE over THUNDER and called the AROUSING and means FOLLOW. Following has supreme success! With LAKE over THUNDER there is splitting action, to tear crack or fissure.   Hex 17 PLAY GUITAR is stimulating, exciting, provoking, pursuing. Clouds can carry as much water as the Mississippi river!

The inside Hexagram 53 is WIND over MOUNTAIN and means DEVELOPMENT, or gradual progress.

PLAY THE FIDDLE
(15)

1	2
SUI	Nuclear: CHIEN
Hexagram 17	Hexagram 53
FOLLOW	**DEVELOPMENT**

Lake over Thunder is Follow

Step up, deflect, parry & punch

STEP-UP, DEFECT, PARRY & PUNCH is Hexagram 16 powerful THUNDER over the receptive EARTH, the I' Ching calls HAPPINESS. Storm clouds and thunder roll across the landscape with arousing shock and awe. Tai Chi shape, STEP-UP, DEFLECT PARRY & PUNCH unleashes the shock & awe energy Hexagram 16 asserts.

Inside, the nuclear Hexagram 39 is WATER over MOUNTAIN, the I' Ching calls OBSTRUCTION, meaning inaccessible. Is this a reference to the power that STEP UP, DEFLECT, PARRY & PUNCH contains or perhaps a warning against poor execution?

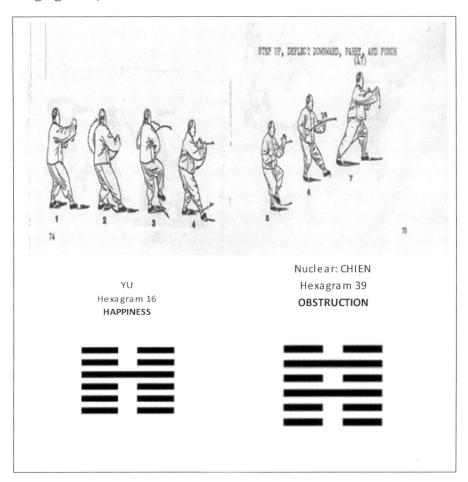

YU
Hexagram 16
HAPPINESS

Nuclear: CHIEN
Hexagram 39
OBSTRUCTION

Thunder over Earth is Enthusiasm

Pick up Needle at Sea Bottom

Pick up NEEDLE AT THE SEA BOTTOM is Hexagram 62 and is called the PREPONDERANCE OF THE SMALL! Trigrams THUNDER is over MOUNTAIN, an idea that a preference for transition must be made before small becomes large. Hexagram 62 NEEDLE AT SEA BOTTOM displays a magnetic energy while retaining compact strength.

The nuclear Hexagram 28 is LAKE over WIND and ironically is called PREPONDERANCE OF THE GREAT meaning when excess is reached it topples on its own weight. The nuclear hexagram appears to hint at maintain center, central equilibrium.

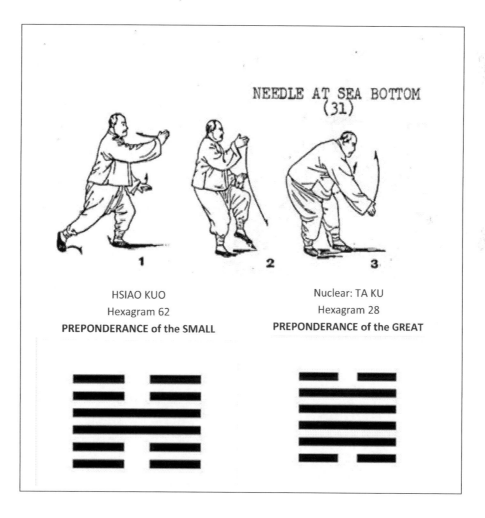

NEEDLE AT SEA BOTTOM
(31)

1   2   3

HSIAO KUO
Hexagram 62
PREPONDERANCE of the SMALL

Nuclear: TA KU
Hexagram 28
PREPONDERANCE of the GREAT

Thunder over Mountain is Preponderance of the Small

Fan through the Back

FAN THROUGH THE BACK is MOUNTAIN over HEAVEN, Hexagram 26 called the TAMING POWER OF THE GREAT. Stand still is chaste innocence and holds heavenly virtues, being genuine and authentic. FAN THROUGH BACK displays strength of heaven and the firm compressed clay of mountain.

The inside or nuclear trigrams are THUNDER over LAKE producing Hexagram 54, the MARRYING MAIDEN; a sensitive compliant and accommodating relationship conditioned on mutual respect. FAN THROUGH THE BACK is supported by THUNDER over HEAVEN but entering requires a little tenderness.

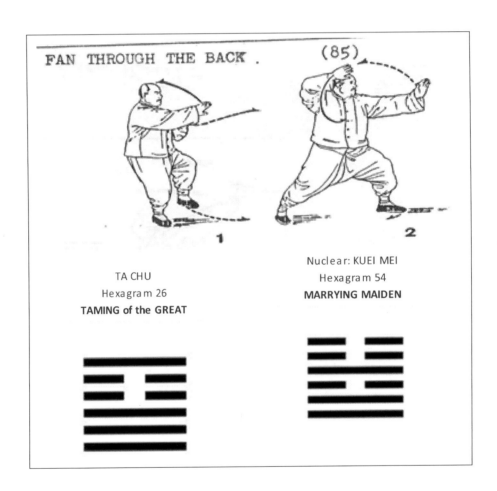

FAN THROUGH THE BACK .   (85)

1

TA CHU
Hexagram 26
TAMING of the GREAT

Nuclear: KUEI MEI
Hexagram 54
MARRYING MAIDEN

2

Mountain over Heaven is called Taming Power of the Great

Back Fist

BACK FIST is Hexagram 28 and is called the PREPONDERANCE OF THE GREAT. LAKE over WIND the I' Ching calls 'PREPONDERANCE OF THE GREAT, carries an image of cloudburst! Meaning things turn in on themselves. When critical mass or excess reaches its peak, its energy becomes spent. When reaching limits or the breaking point, best to yield, submit, relent to the passing of greatness.

The inside nuclear Hexagram 1 is HEAVEN the creative, celestial movements set in motion. Very little stands against heaven.

TURN AND CHOP OPPON WITH FIST
(46)

TA KUO
Hexagram 28
PREPONDERANCE of the GREAT

Nuclear: CH'IEN
Hexagram 1
the CREATIVE

Lake over Wind is Preponderance of the Great

Snake flicks out its Tongue

SNAKE FLICKS OUT ITS TONGUE is Hexagram 19 called LOVE. EARTH over LAKE gives an image of a bowl, a vessel, maybe a gathering or coming together. Hexagram 19 WHITE SNAKE FLICKS TONGUE displays a gentle penetrating energy that sinks into a firm but dynamic base.

The nuclear Hexagram 24 is EARTH over THUNDER, called RETURN and breakthrough; the RETURN indicates a revival, a turning point, going out and coming in without error, to and fro returns follows the Way.

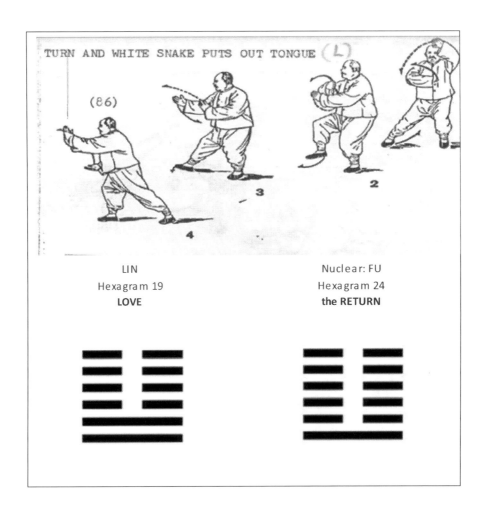

Earth over Lake is called Love

Withdraw & Push

WITHDRAW & PUSH is Hexagram 50. Fire over Wind, and is called the CAULDRON; the gentle penetrating wind whipping up fire: clinging, consuming and bonding, sticky. Hexagram 50 is WITHDRAW & PUSH. It is propelling energy arising from sticky hands.

Its nuclear or hidden is Hexagram 43, LAKE OVER HEAVEN and is called DETERMINATION, meaning resoluteness, unfaltering, steadfast, displacement and single-minded.

TWIST HAND OUT   WITHDRAW AND PUSH   (18)

1   2   3   4

TING
Hexagram 50
the **CAULDRON**

Nuclear: KUAI
Hexagram 43
DETERMINATION

Fire over Wind is a Cauldron

Apparent Close

   APPARRENT CLOSE is Hexagram 36 and is called Darkening of the Light. It displays inaccessibility, effortlessness, centering.

   The nuclear Hexagram 40 is THUNDER over WATER and is called DELIVERANCE and liberation; meaning obstacles removed, out of danger, untangling situations, and release.

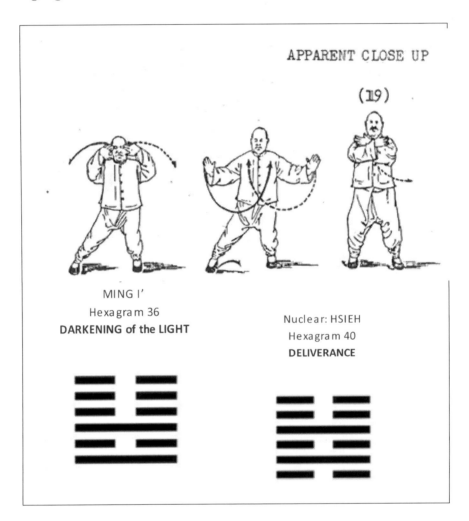

APPARENT CLOSE UP

(19)

MING I'
Hexagram 36
DARKENING of the LIGHT

Nuclear: HSIEH
Hexagram 40
DELIVERANCE

Earth over Fire is Darkening of the Light

Embrace Tiger Return to Mountain

EMBRACE TIGER RETURN TO MOUNTAIN is Hexagram 52 called KEEP STILL and is mountain over mountain. It displays an arresting influence that is cautious, unwavering, and unyielding, check mate. Stand your ground.

The nuclear Hexagram 40 is THUNDER over WATER, called DELIVERANCE and means a return to stability, liberation, and release.

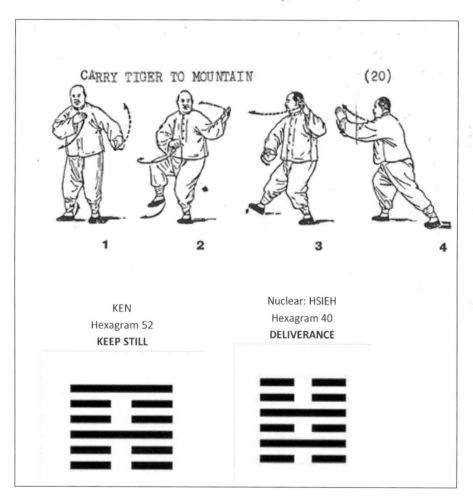

CARRY TIGER TO MOUNTAIN   (20)

1   2   3   4

KEN
Hexagram 52
KEEP STILL

Nuclear: HSIEH
Hexagram 40
DELIVERANCE

Mountain over Mountain is Keep Still

Diagonal Single whip

SINGLE WHIP is LAKE over FIRE and is called REVOLUTION and metamorphosis because the joyous LAKE over consuming FIRE brings fundamental change. The image creates of a lake of lava. It is fundamental change. Hexagram 49 SINGLE WHIP is consuming, whipping, boiling, swirling, tossing, seething & moving.

The nuclear Hexagram 44 is called TEMTATION and COMING TO MEET. It is the marriage of HEAVEN and WIND/WOOD cryptically warning that it is not advisable to marry powerful maidens. There is a singular magnetic attraction but relationship will not last.

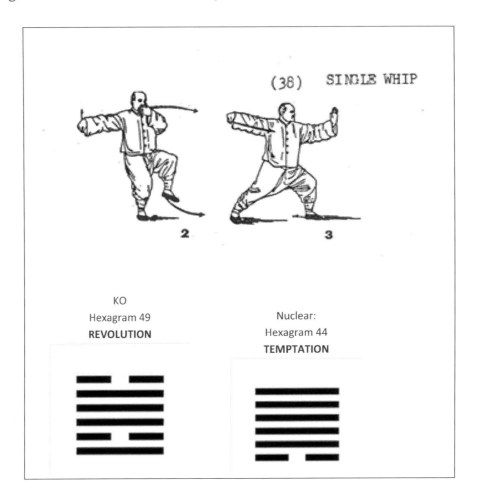

KO
Hexagram 49
REVOLUTION

Nuclear:
Hexagram 44
TEMPTATION

Lake over Fire is called Revolution

Fist below elbow

FIST BELOW ELBOW is Hexagram 27 has Mountain over Thunder displaying an image of wide open jaws, meaning providing nourishment, prudence and temperance.

The Nuclear Hexagram 2 is Earth the Receptive, a magnetic and attractive force.

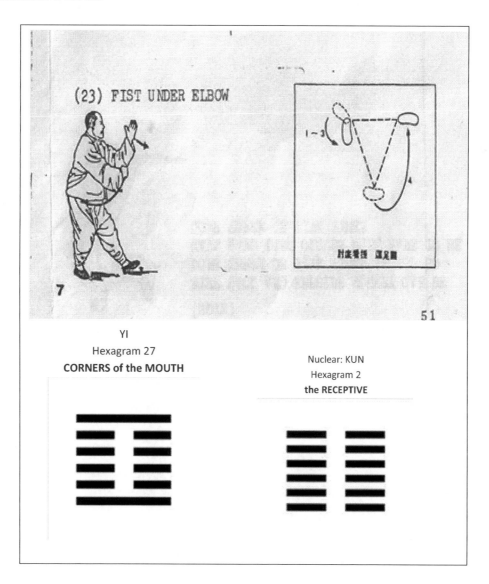

YI
Hexagram 27
CORNERS of the MOUTH

Nuclear: KUN
Hexagram 2
the RECEPTIVE

Mountain over Thunder is Corners of the Mouth

Step back and repulse monkey

STEP BACK TO Repulse Monkey IS Hexagram 33 with Mountain below the heavens and means RETREAT. STEP BACK TO REPULSE MONKEY is a strategic withdrawal, to reconnect. Movement enjoys compression and strength of Heaven. Neutralize.

The nuclear Hexagram is I' Ching 44 and means COMING TO MEET, a cryptic message about a furtive unseen danger is poised to seize power.

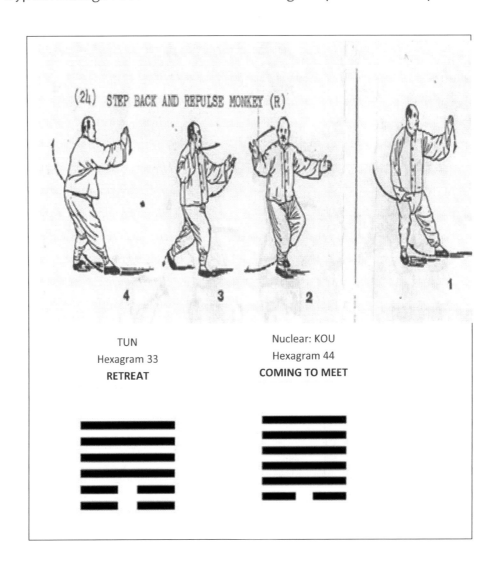

TUN
Hexagram 33
RETREAT

Nuclear: KOU
Hexagram 44
COMING TO MEET

Heaven over Mountain is Retreat

Diagonal Flying

DIAGONAL FLYING is I' Chin g Hexagram 59 with trigram Wind, the gentle moving over trigram Water this is called DISPERSION.   The idea conjures images of dissolution displacement, diffusion, disintegration. Hexagram 59 WIND OVER WATER is splitting energy entering by expansion and penetration.

Inside Hexagram 27 the I' Ching calls the CORNERS OF THE MOUTH so called for looks like open jaws for nourishment, and implies temperance.

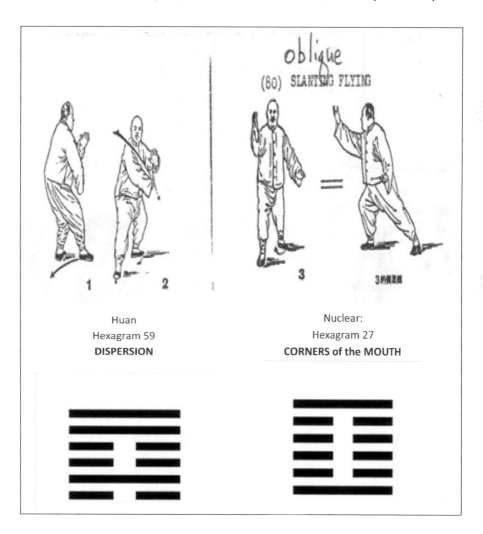

Wind over Water is Dispersion

Cloud Hands

WAVE HANDS LIKE CLOUDS is Hexagram 3 Water over Thunder, producing an image of clouds & Thunder and means DIFFICULTY AT THE BEGINNING or growing pains, initial obstacles overcome. WAVE HANDS LIKE CLOUDS is undulating fluid movements with penetrating strength.

Coincidently, the nuclear Hexagram 23 the I' Ching calls SPLITTING APART and means submit to avoid action.

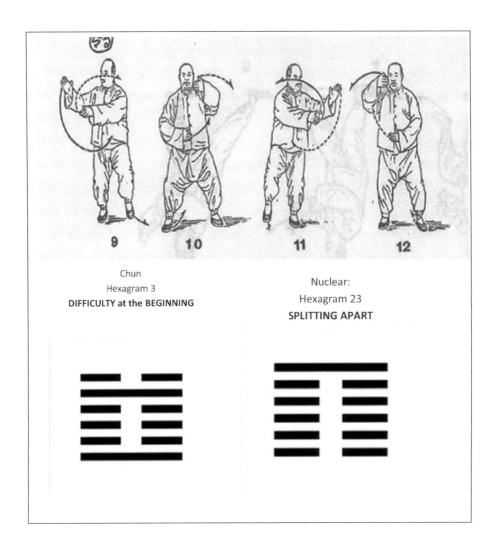

Chun
Hexagram 3
DIFFICULTY at the BEGINNING

Nuclear:
Hexagram 23
SPLITTING APART

Water over Thunder is Difficulty at the Beginning

Snake Creeps Down

SNAKE CREEPS DOWN is Hexagram 7, Earth over Water. An image of an aquifer, a reservoir, stored strength with discipline, like an ARMY, invisible 'til needed. SNAKE CREEPS DOWN displays fluid slipping away, vanishing, hiding, falling away without warning, attractive magnetic energy.

Its nuclear Hexagram 24 is called the RETURN by I' Ching and means like a turning point, a sudden reversal. It should be effortless smooth natural movement, not by force.

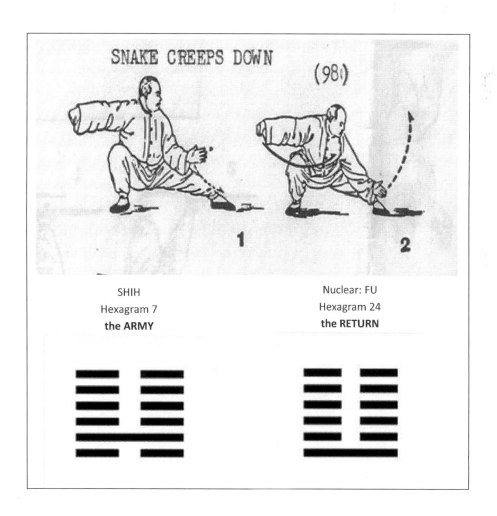

Earth over Water means the ARMY

Golden Pheasant Stands on One Leg

GOLDEN PHEASANT STANDS ON ONE LEG is Hexagram 61 Wind over Lake the I' Ching calls the INNER TRUTH. Wind stirs Lake; there is an advantage in being sincere and correct.

Inside Hexagram 27 is CORNERS OF THE MOUTH, meaning nourishment; regulates speech and controls eating and drinking.

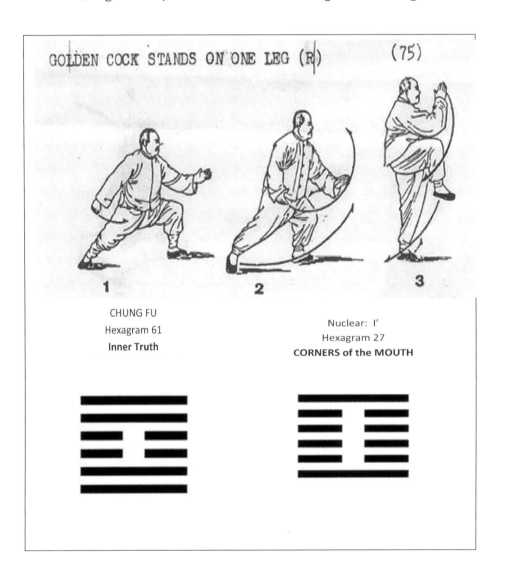

GOLDEN COCK STANDS ON ONE LEG (R)   (75)

1   2   3

CHUNG FU
Hexagram 61
Inner Truth

Nuclear: I'
Hexagram 27
CORNERS of the MOUTH

Wind over Lake is Inner Truth

High Pat on Horse

HIGH PAT ON THE HORSE is Hexagram 56 and called the WANDERER. Fire on Mountain, an image of fast moving grass fire; doesn't linger, image of a wanderer, a traveler, home is the road. Hex 56 is transition and HIGH PAT ON HORSE exhibits steadfast clinging energy like fire on a mountain.

Nuclear Hexagram 28 is PREPONDERANCE OF THE GREAT meaning things turn in on themselves, there is a breaking point.

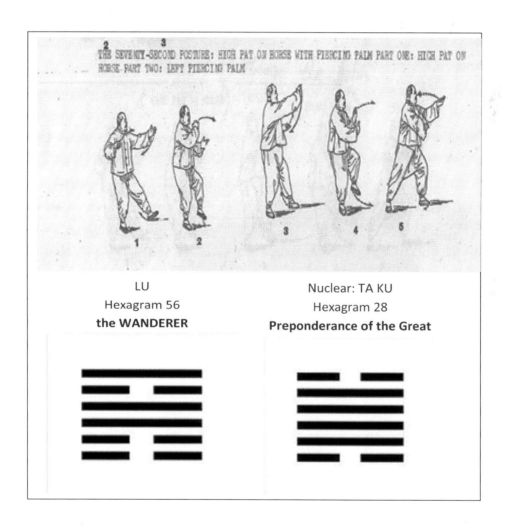

Fire over Mountain is called the Wanderer

Separate Right & Left Foot

SEPARATE LEFT & RIGHT FOOT is THUNDER over THUNDER; it is hexagram 51 called the AROUSING. Thunder is arousing, startling, and sudden. From startling movement comes SHOCK, uh-oh! Then comes ha-ha for fear is good for joy & merriment. Hexagram 51 SEPARATE FOOT is shock of thunder and quick discharge of yang energy.

The nuclear Hexagram 39 is WATER over MOUNTAIN;   I' Ching meaning is OBSTRUCTION, inaccessible, blocked.

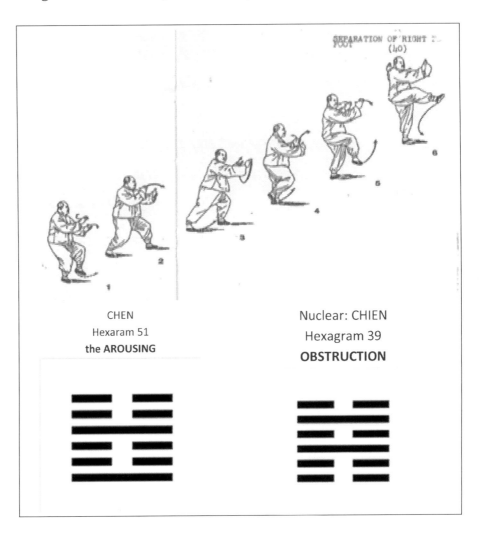

CHEN
Hexaram 51
the AROUSING

Nuclear: CHIEN
Hexagram 39
OBSTRUCTION

Thunder over Thunder is called the Arousing

Turn around kick with heel

TURN AROUND AND KICK WITH HEEL is hexagram 25 HEAVEN over THUNDER and means INNOCENCE. The misfortune in missing a target lies in opposing the Way. Heaven over Thunder is the Image of innocence, moral, pure, lacking guile. Innocence and correctness is progress.

Inside or nuclear Hexagram 53 is called DEVELOPMENT ascribed to WIND over MOUNTAIN and means there is gradual progress in learning.

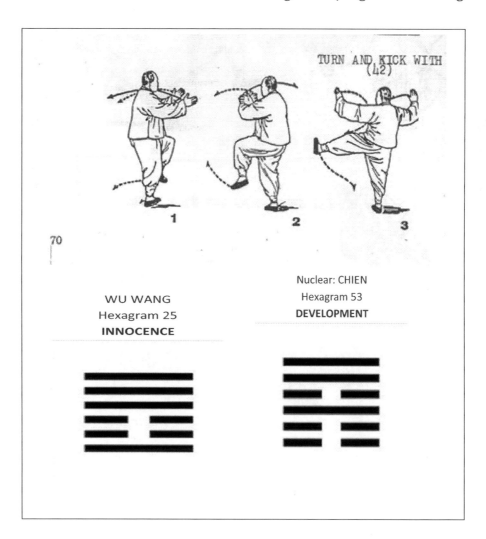

TURN AND KICK WITH
(42)

1   2   3

70

WU WANG
Hexagram 25
INNOCENCE

Nuclear: CHIEN
Hexagram 53
DEVELOPMENT

Heaven over Thunder is Innocence

Low Punch to Groin

   LOW PUNCH TO GROIN Is hexagram 15; EARTH over MOUNTAIN; a mountain hiding in the EARTH, an image of modesty, moderation, timidity. Hexagram 15 is LOW PUNCH TO GROIN, resulting when one unmovable meets another results are humbling.

   Nuclear Hexagram 40 is THUNDER over WATER meaning DELIVERANCE.

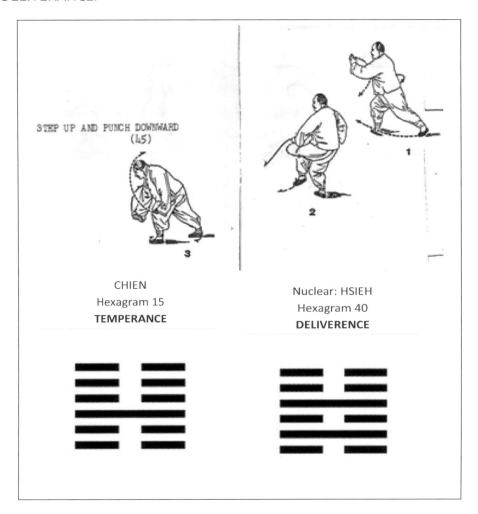

CHIEN
Hexagram 15
TEMPERANCE

Nuclear: HSIEH
Hexagram 40
DELIVERENCE

Earth over Mountain is Temperance

Wind Blows through Ears

WIND BLOWS THROUGH EARS is hexagram 21, FIRE over THUNDER is called BITING THROUGH. Without justice there is no harmony. BITING THROUGH is breakthrough, yielding receives success, a place of honor, when timing is right, let justice be administered.

Nuclear Hexagram 39 is OBSTRUCTION the inaccessible WATER over MOUNTAIN, waterfalls. Note the hollowed fists, beware of ego.

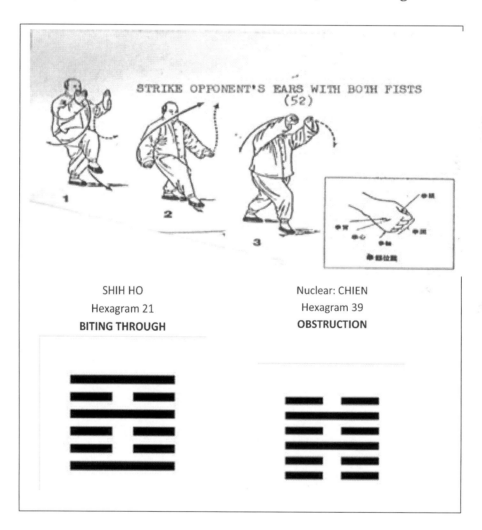

Fire over Thunder is Biting Through

Fair Lady Works at Shuttle

FAIR LADY WORKS AT SHUTTLE is hexagram 60, WATER over LAKE and means LIMITATION. Constraint or limitation is an image of containment, regulation. Hexagram 60 FAIR LADY WORKS AT SHUTTLE is limitation, contain expansion. Disruptive natural forces beyond control.

Nuclear Hexagram is DIFFICULTY AT THE BEGINNING referring to giving birth or similar labor. Be mindful of central equilibrium.

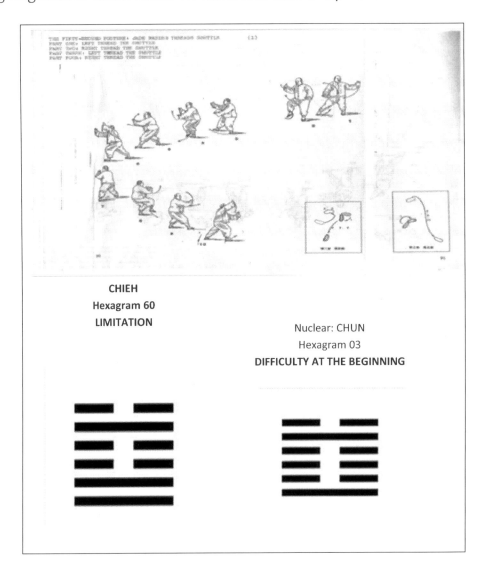

CHIEH
Hexagram 60
LIMITATION

Nuclear: CHUN
Hexagram 03
DIFFICULTY AT THE BEGINNING

Water over Lake is Limitation

Step up to Seven Stars

STEP UP TO SEVEN STARS is hexagram 55 is THUNDER over FIRE, an image of fullness, and ABUNDANCE, expansion everywhere. Here clinging FIRE meets arousing THUNDER in a kinetic experience.

Inside Hexagram 28 is LAKE over WIND is called PREPONDERANCE OF THE GREAT meaning things turn in on themselves. Be aware when excess is great it falls.

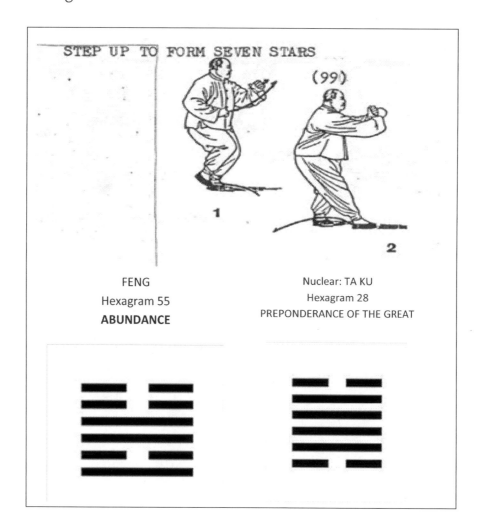

FENG

Hexagram 55

ABUNDANCE

Nuclear: TA KU

Hexagram 28

PREPONDERANCE OF THE GREAT

Thunder over Fire is Abundance

Step back & ride the Tiger

STEP BACK & RIDE THE TIGER, Hexagram 53 is WIND over MOUNTAIN; an image of gradual progress and means DEVELOPMENT. Hexagram 53 STEP BACK AND RIDE TIGER be still as MOUNTAIN gently penetrating like the WIND.

Nuclear Hexagram 64 is FIRE over WATER! And is called BEFORE COMPLETION and means work is not yet finished.

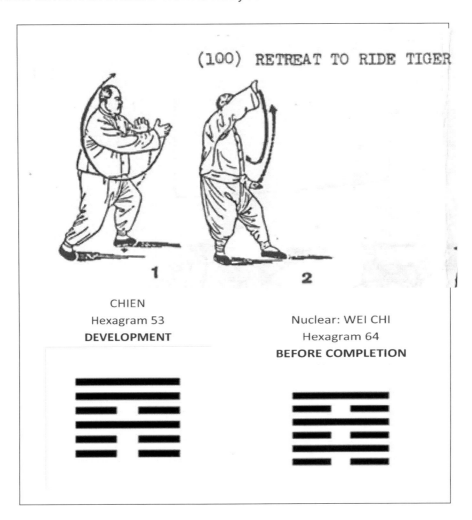

(100) RETREAT TO RIDE TIGER

1

2

CHIEN
Hexagram 53
DEVELOPMENT

Nuclear: WEI CHI
Hexagram 64
BEFORE COMPLETION

Wind over Mountain is Development

Turn around Kick with Lotus

TURN AROUND AND KICK WITH A LOTUS is Hexagram 64 and has FIRE over WATER, very powerful, yet Hexagram 64 is called BEFORE COMPLETION there are things yet undone, tread lightly when on ice.   The last of I' Ching hexagrams, a reminder to be cautious, there are no conclusions, Murphy's Law is operating here.

Inside our nuclear Hexagram 53 is WIND over MOUNTAIN which the I' Ching calls DEVELOPMENT and cautions progress is gradual.

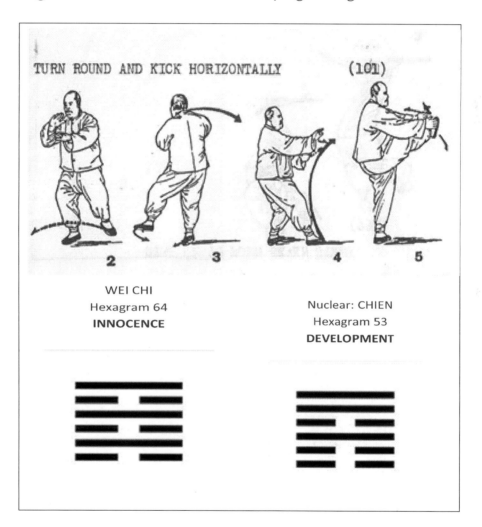

Heaven over Thunder is called Innocence

Bend bow & Shoot Tiger

BEND BOW AND SHOOT TIGER is THUNDER over WATER, the Abyss. Arousing the Abyss, tensions are released; movement brings clouds, rain, deliverance, liberation.

Nuclear Hexagram 63 is AFTER COMPLETION the transition of order to chaos, a hidden influence. Situations appear stable but prepare for disorder and embark in a new direction.

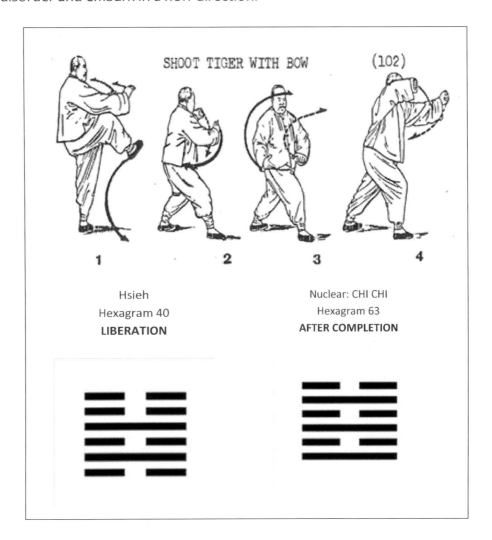

SHOOT TIGER WITH BOW   (102)

1   2   3   4

Hsieh
Hexagram 40
LIBERATION

Nuclear: CHI CHI
Hexagram 63
AFTER COMPLETION

Thunder over Water is Liberation

Withdraw and push

WITHDRAW & PUSH is Hexagram 50. Fire over Wind, and is called the CAULDRON; the gentle penetrating wind whipping up fire: clinging, consuming and bonding, sticky. Hexagram 50 is WITHDRAW & PUSH. It is propelling energy arising from sticky hands.

Its nuclear or hidden is Hexagram 43 called DETERMINATION, meaning resoluteness, unfaltering, steadfast, displacement and single-mindedness.

TWIST HAND OUT   WITHDRAW AND PUSH   (18)

TING	Nuclear: KUAI
Hexagram 50	Hexagram 43
the CAULDRON	**BREAKTHROUGH**

Fire over Wind is called the Cauldron

Crossing Hands

CROSSING HANDS is Earth over Fire, conjures an image of smothering a fire, a darkening of light, a sun setting. Hexagram 36 CROSS HANDS is symbolized by Earth extinguishing Fire.

Inside Hexagram 40 is THUNDER over WATER the I' Ching calls DELIVERANCE; obstacles removed and are out of danger.

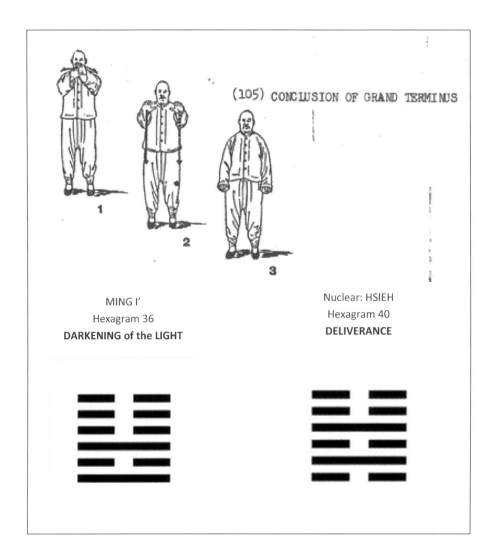

(105) CONCLUSION OF GRAND TERMINUS

MING I'
Hexagram 36
DARKENING of the LIGHT

Nuclear: HSIEH
Hexagram 40
DELIVERANCE

Earth over Fire is Darkening of Light

Taiji

Musings

In looking after your life and following the way, gather spirit.
Gather spirit early...

-Tao te Ching

Tai Chi Ch'uan is merely a vehicle we use to learn to move in space.

The stated goal of Tai Chi ch'uan is immortality. The rewards of Tai Chi ch'uan are vitality and longevity.

Tai Chi Ch'uan Classics, the Song of Thirteen Postures has two admonitions: "you can practice Tai Chi your whole life, but if you practice incorrectly, it is all for naught. "to enter the door you must be taught orally". Traditionally, Tai Chi Ch'uan was passed along from father to son.

Being mindful of correct body mechanics in any human activity is critical to balance, coordination and function.

Correct movement means Tai Chi Ch'uan is natural and balanced. So sitting, standing, squatting and walking and lifting really are produced naturally by the body, supported by the earth and are effortless. To 'do' tai chi wrong, just add stress.

When a body moves naturally it is eloquent, fluid and articulate, graceful.

This means no stressful discomfort is felt on neck, shoulders, spine, hips, knees, ankles or toes. Arms are carried by the trunk of the body and should not move independent of the trunk of your body.

Being mindful of your movements is all the concentration you need. Do not allow your mind to wander. Try doing less rather than more. Feel the natural weight, flow and movement of your body as it moves in space. Your body's natural intelligence will find central equilibrium and relax.

Secrets of Tai Chi Ch'uan

For solo, tsui shou or san shou practice

(**CENTER** yourself) Head is suspended above. INHALE gently into your dantien, release tension with exhale.

Your foot is 'rooted' when three nail points on your foot are firm on the ground (see William C.C. Chen, ART of TAI CHI CHUAN).

Be aware which full and empty, not just your legs but whole body (substantial and insubstantial).

Arms and movement are **CIRCULAR** carried by the trunk of your body, arms do not move independent of body.

Entire body moves as one unit; **coordination**.

Sung Qua or RELAX sacrum, work your legs. Arms, legs are proportionate giving the entire body **BALANCE**.

Be mindful of chi-energy, harmony is balance between yin-yang

Lead with your mind. **Concentrate**.

Three Don'ts:
Don't push back
don't pull away
never by force

Dr. Tao Ping Siang

Bagua & Thirteen Kinetic Postures of Tai Chi Ch'uan

There are **Five steps** and **Eight gates** (or directions) that characterize the **thirteen kinetic postures of Tai chi ch'uan** and are illustrated on the **Bagua**.

North comes force of **Winter, cold, water, kidney**
South brings the force of **Summer, heat, fire, heart**
East brings **Spring, growth, the wind, wood, liver**
West creates the force of **Autumn, Dry, metal, lung**

The 8 Gates (directions):

Four cardinal gates

1. **North**..........Peng..........Ward-off..........Ch'ien..............Heaven
2. **South**..........Lu..............Roll-away.........Kun...............Earth
3. **East**.............Ji..............Press.............Kan.................Water
4. **West**..........An.............Push.............Li...............Fire

The Four diagonal gates

5. **Northeast**..............Tsai.........Pull-down.......Sun........Wind
6. **Southeast**..............Kao.........Shoulder.........Ken......Mountain
7. **Northwest**..............Zhou.......Elbow strike....Tui..........Lake
8. **Southwest**.............Li............Split..............Chen......Thunder

FIVE STEPS are the sequence called **'grasp sparrows' tail'** and is the core of tai chi and bagua movements. **Grasp Sparrows Tail** incorporate the **Five Steps** and are essential to tai chi ch'uan. Each step correlates to one of **Wu Xing or Five Elements theory**.

Movement	Element
1. Center	Earth
2. Right step	Metal
3. Left step	Wood
4. Forward step	Fire
5. Rear step	Water

Tai Chi Ch'uan movements are always relaxed and natural, maintaining central equilibrium at all times. Step like a cat, be still as a mountain, sink like water, move like the wind.

Waist down moves like water and clouds from waist up.

The eight gates plus our five steps are the thirteen kinetic postures of Tai Chi Ch'uan. Signature postures being Ward-off, Roll back, Press, Push or Peng, Lu Ji and An, respectively.

Mind & Breath are King and Queen, the bones and muscle are the court.   -Tai Chi Classics

脚分右（步换）身转（手上）55

Seven Chi Meridians and Psychic centers

As the body moves relaxed and slowly, the seven chi meridians or psychic centers are activated stimulate your sympathetic and parasympathetic body systems.

1. **Bai Hui** ……..…. Crown………..A thousand meetings

2. **Ming Men**……..…..Lumbar…..……………. the Gate of life

3. **Qi Hai** …..……..… Dantien…..…..……..….the Sea of Chi

4. **Lao Gong** …..…..…..R palm …..…..…..……..Palace of Toil

5. **Lao Gong** …..…..…...Left palm …..…..…..…..Palace of Toil

6. **Yong Quan** …..…….. Right ball of foot …..Bubbling Well

7. **Yong Quan** …..……..Left ball of foot……. Bubbling Well

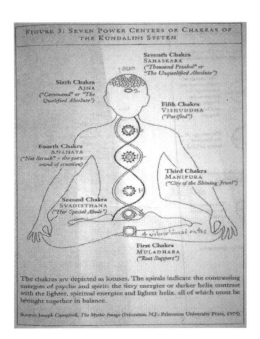

Ref: image from Roslyn Bruyere WHEELS OF LIGHT

The Nine Pearls*

1. Ankle
2. Knee
3. Hips
4. Sacrum
5. Lumbar
6. Thoracic
7. Shoulders
8. Elbows
9. Palms; wrists & fingers

Meditation

Grandmaster William C.C. Chen says the slow movements of tai chi ch'uan is a "silent brain exercise" and total body communication.

The difference between sleep and meditation is, when asleep, we forget our name. Meditation alters the electrical activity of your brain. BETA waves improve concentration. GAMMA waves are intense focus. ALPHA waves calm the nervous system, lower blood pressure and heart rate. The brain waves reduce production of stress hormones and promote relaxation. THETA waves promote a tranquil state promoting calm and balance. THETA waves encourage creativity, increases memory focus and problem solving skills. DELTA waves are associated with deepest sleep and healing. The moving meditation of tai chi ch'uan increases oxygen rich blood to the brain.

" The Whole Body moves as one in Great Harmony" says Dr. Tao, Ping Siang during one Spring in 1998 Seattle.

The Three Nails

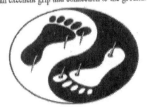
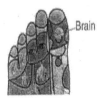

The three points of the three nails are important components that provide a Tai Chi player with an excellent grip and connection to the ground.

Brain

Two books written by Grandmaster William C.C. Chen are worthy manuals for Tai Chi players; <u>The Body Mechanics of Tai Chi Ch'uan</u> or <u>The Art Tai of 60 Movements Yang style Short form.</u>

Crucial to developing good Tai Chi ch'uan is a solid root or foundation that gives you strong legs and feet firm on the ground. Crucial to developing good Tai Chi ch'uan is a solid root or foundation that gives you strong legs and feet firm on the ground., so too, with the information you absorb to attain insight into the chi-energy behind the posture.

Central equilibrium is possible when your legs possess the strength to carry yourself. Your foot is firm or rooted when all three nails touch the ground, activating thigh and groin muscle.

Grandmaster William C. C. Chen's Body Mechanics of Tai Chi Ch'uan** reveals the importance of body mechanics from the toes of your feet, legs, muscles, breathing, heart and organs stay healthy and provide oxygen and nutrients and elimination of wastes, toxins and carbon dioxide from the body.

Tai Chi Ch'uan as a daily exercise is very healthy; it cultivates breathing, our coordination, and balance and blood circulation.

Dantien

A very special place in our bodies is the dantien or tan–tien (pronounced "dawn- tee-in'). The dantien is called Sea of Chi. Movement begins here. Dantien is where we sense and feel the center of our body is located. Its location is approximately an inch or two in front of the sacrum or holy bone and three fingers below your belly button toward the center of your body. Five bones are fused here creating a bowl. The ability to sung-qua lives here. Concentrate your mind and breathe here.

I am reminded that located above the dantien is another energy center, above and in front of the Ming Men (DU4), the area of the solar plexus. Yoga people call it "the jewel at the center of the lotus blossom. Also called Solar Plexus and third chakra, where life and vitality flows.

Below, Professor Cheng Man Ching illustrates that sung-qua is accomplished by softening the jewel center by hollowing the chest and plucking the back, compared to Grandmaster William C. C. Chen sacrum flex and softening, dantien follows.

Photos:

Cheng Man-Ch'ing's Advanced Tai hi Form Instruction by Douglas Wile
William C.C. Chen Grandmaster Body Mechanics of Tai Chi Ch'uan

Circumspection or full circle

Tai Chi Ch'uan and Chi Kung are cultivation arts, vehicles we use to gain strength and balance. Especially balance in our life; at the same time, we learn skills to confront most unpleasant situations with aplomb.

But, there is something very unique about the practice of the internal arts, that are in danger of being forgotten by today's Chi kung, Tai Chi, Bagua, Tsing I' & Lei Hu Ba Fa players. That is, their chi roots are in the I' Ching. It is the oldest of the Chinese Classics.

Taoism, the I' Ching, Wu Xing, and YIN/YANG theory follow nature, and are much older than Tai Chi Ch'uan or its sister arts that have inspired correct behavior in people for millennia.

Virtually all serious books on Tai Chi ch'uan, Bagua, Tsing I', and styles of martial arts and you find this symbol, the bagua.

Why did the ancients think bagua, the eight-trigrams and the I' Ching so important to the internal arts (nei gong)? And why should we care as inheritors of this grand art.

Lao Tzu knew that the I' Ching had a greater significance than just a book of changes, an oracle at best. Lao Tzu may have realized the book of wisdom as a cultivation tool. The art of Tai Chi Ch'uan is in the understanding (intuiting?) the I' Ching and tempering ourselves as we test it through natural law. The difference between knowledge and wisdom is in its application. We may enjoy deeper appreciation for living within natures' harmony.

"Elements of nature are ephemeral and that, once aware of this, we must conduct our lives accordingly.... Healing Ourselves by Naboru Muramoto*

The timeless I' Ching and the vivifying effects of tai chi ch'uan are gifts of good conduct and longevity for mankind.

Tai Chi meditation can be thought of as an alchemical process, "...to reach the highest state of consciousness which transcends the bonds of mortality that cramp ordinary existence" explains Master Da Liu, in his book <u>Tai Chi Ch'uan and I' Ching.</u>

The stated goal of Tai Chi Ch'uan is immortality!

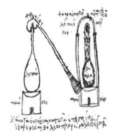

Master Da Liu says that when metal is transformed by alchemy (chemistry), it is heated in a flask or crucible, refined, passed to another flask then repeated several times. The new purified materials are formed into something new.

Master Liu explains, "The body of the student is the alchemist laboratory. The psychic center or spiritual organs of the body have the function of the flasks in alchemical distillation. The breath of the meditator can be compared to the bellows and the psychic fluids to the purified elixir which is passed from one flask to the other in the laboratory."

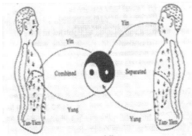

Illustration from the <u>Tao of Tai Chi Ch'uan</u> by Master Jou, Sung-Hwa

Master Da Liu continues, "As meditation begins ching or sexual energy rises up to a point about an inch and a half below the naval. This may be compared to heating a cauldron on a stove creating steam. This point is known as the dantien.

At the dantien the first purification cycle begins; sexual energy transmuted to chi. This cycle is called little heaven circulation; which is elegantly described in the OPENING movement of Tai Chi Ch'uan."

"Greater heavenly circulation is a purification process that passes your chi through all of the psychic centers. Jing has already been transformed by breath and heat during lesser heavenly current".

Tai Chi Ch'uan is a cultivation art because Greater Heavenly circulation is captured in the Tai Chi Ch'uan postures. The I' Ching assists in building an attitude of right behavior for a life seeking love, peace, harmony, health and happiness.

It is less important for one to know the philosophies, mechanisms and alchemical processes of tai chi and I' Ching , the TAO just follows nature. Daily practice will suffice to gain strong health bodies.

In following Tao or nature you need only stand in your own two feet, experience the plumb of your body supported by earth, breathe deeply the atmosphere into your dantien and connect your five senses to resonate with Nature.

For the tai chi player, yielding is preferable to confronting a force head on. This can be done without surrender. You are equipped with defensive skills that enable you to protect yourself. The strength of tai chi is in the fact that two objects cannot occupy the same spot.

Competition in tai chi ch'uan is useful in tai chi practice. Pushing hands, tsui shou and san shou, aside from being fun, their essential worth is found in participation. Testing your art, and exposes you to yourself. Ego is something confronted early in training. Cultivate spirit early. The preponderance of small precedes greatness.

The correct mental, emotional attitude and good vibes (chi-energy) in Tai Chi Ch'uan & Chi Kung are the same for meditation, quiet and relaxed.

The correct mental, emotional attitude and good vibes (chi-energy) in Tai Chi Ch'uan & Chi Kung is the same for meditation; quiet and relaxed.

Tai Chi Ch'uan is defensive action. Soft overcomes the hard by yielding first. In competition as well as in play we meet ourselves in your partner. Your partner generally mirrors your true attitude about confronting life.

A warriors' code is 'Last Man Standing'.

A word about empty hands fighting (tui shou, san shou), I tell you, in a fight where the attitude is 'last-man-standing'; the fight is in the heart where battle rages and actually takes place. Technique is cold comfort here. There are many martial schools, many teachers, ideas and notions about fighting (survival). Some equip you with good tools others not so good, your protection and safety is your responsibility. I believe Tai Chi ch'uan instincts can provide a decent defensive response. Anything more and other martial skills need to be acquired.

Tai chi principles do not change, even in combat. Not by force, follow.

Chi-energy (be it intentional or unintentional) is another word for information carried throughout our dynamic world at all times, evoking emotional responses in the form of fights or flights as we react to our environment. Energy always carries a charge.

Words, sounds and gestures carry charged information by the energy within and behind them. Our very comprehension of words, sounds and gestures produce images, tastes , smells and feelings carry information. Any one of our five senses can elicit a wide range of memories, emotions and responses.

Our minds are fluid, never still, nebulous chi-energy, it is YIN. All stuff in the universe is possible. But Our bodies are set into flesh, it is YANG, WYSIWYG (what you see is what you get).

As ideas inure and concretize into visibility they shift into event and patterns you have entertained in your mind.

For negative energy, Tai Chi offers a neutral response. In stead of the urge to fight or flight; we can Yield to the incoming force. Take the middle ground, a neutral response.

Tai Chi Ch'uan is a practical defensive martial art, but more importantly, Tai Chi Ch'uan is an excellent regimen for vibrant body health, and youthful mind well into old age.

Within the Book of Changes (I' Ching), we now know that the changing lines within bagua give structure to I' Ching hexagrams. The hexagram structures are constructed by Chi-energy, informed and interpreted into structure. Hexagrams are not so much understood but intuited or felt internally. You can see that there can be a myriad of changes behind any posture by way of its chi-energy; though the outward appearances remain unchanged.

I hope that Tai Chi Chuan, the Chinese Classics, and the I' Ching offer perspective on how to play with Tai Chi Ch'uan, and the lessons presented return us to a time when chi-energy was important to our practice.

Enjoy relaxation as you never thought possible. Maintain core strength and suppleness. Marshall low stress levels or increase performance stress without the dis-stress. Practice Tai Chi Ch'uan for longevity and be forever young.

Be gentle with your-self, and one another.

Ben Noma

I respectfully dedicate my book to my teachers Dr. Tao Ping Siang, Grandmaster William C.C. Chen, and Professor Hsu Shan Tung and T.Y. Pang, all of whom with great patience, guided my tai chi journey. I wish to include the many dedicated students to the art of tai chi ch'uan without which I could not learn. And many patient classmates that have tempered my volatile spirit without which I would not have learned.

Resource

The Illustrations are Grandmaster Yang Cheng-Fu circa 1973 Tai Chi Ch'uan
book authored by Yang Cheng-Fu and Professor Cheng Man-Ching

Body Mechanics of Tai Chi Ch'uan
William C.C. Chen Grandmaster Taiji
1973 New York

Form Defines Energy: Essence of Feng Shui
Professor Shan-Tung Hsu PhD. Taiji Master
2014 Seattle

Cheng Man-Ch'ing's Advanced Tai Chi Form Instruction
compiled and translated by Douglas Wile
1985 New York

A Little beneath the Surface of the Tai Ji Quan Classic
Ping-Siang Tao Taiji Grandmaster
Taipei, Taiwan 1994

TAO of Feng Shui
Prof. Shan-Tung Hsu PhD. Taiji Master
Blue Mountain Feng Shui Institute
Seattle 1999

On Tai Chi Chuan
T.Y. Pang, Taiji Master
Azalea Press 1987

Lao Tzu Tao Te Ching
Ursula K. Leguin
Shambala Press 1997

Tai Chi Ch'uan & Meditation
Master Da Liu
New York 1986

Tai Chi Ch'uan and I Ching: Choreography of Body and Mind
Master Da Liu
New York 1972

The I Ching or Book of Changes
Richard Wilhelm
Bollinger Foundation

The TAO of Tai Chi Chuan
Jou, Tsung-Hwa, Taiji Master
Taiwan 1980

Healing Ourselves
Naboru Muramoto
Avon Books 1973

The Water Wizard
Victor Schauberger

The Essence of Tai Chi Ch'uan
Inner Research Institute School of Tai Chi Ch'uan

Lao Tzu Te Tao Ching Ma-Wang-Tui text
Robert G. Hendricks

Yang Family Secret Transmissions
Douglas Wile
New York 1983

ISBN: 9 7985 54498 626

Ben Noma
PO Box 14003
Settle, WA 98115

Made in the USA
Columbia, SC
01 July 2022

62561105R00061